The
CHURCH'S
MINISTRY

T. W. MANSON
*Rylands Professor of Biblical Criticism and Exegesis
in the University of Manchester*

With a Preface by

HENRY SLOANE COFFIN
*President Emeritus of
Union Theological Seminary, New York*

Philadelphia
THE WESTMINSTER PRESS

PRINTED IN THE UNITED STATES OF AMERICA

PREFACE

IN RECENT negotiations for Church union no subject has proved more of an obstacle than that of basic differences in the conception of the Church and of its ministry. These same differences emerged sharply at the meeting in Amsterdam where the World Council of Churches was inaugurated, and prevented the delegates from joining in a common celebration of the Lord's Supper. The "catholic" and the "evangelical" views of the Church and of the ministry are difficult to reconcile, perhaps cannot be entirely reconciled. The "catholic" view sees the Church divinely constituted with a particular order of ministers, in which the bishops are the successors of the original apostles, and are alone vested with power to ordain other ministers. Such ministers only who possess this apostolic succession may properly administer the Holy Communion. The "evangelical" view sees the Church an apostolic fellowship of followers of Christ, in which all believers in him are called to be priests, and to them all is entrusted the apostolic ministry of bringing the Gospel to mankind. Within the Church Christ bestows on certain disciples gifts of leadership, which the Church recognizes, and therefore commis-

sions these individuals to various ministries. In the
" catholic " view the bishops are primary and through
them the Church is continued from century to century.
In the " evangelical " view the company of believers
in Christ is primary; they are the Body of Christ, and
in them the living Christ age after age dwells, and
leads and empowers them for the continuation of his
work. Happily, evangelicals do not deny the reality
of the ministry of those who hold the " catholic " conception of the Church; they gladly partake of the
Holy Communion with them, provided the " catholics " will permit such fellowship. But the " catholics "
usually feel that their ministry alone is apostolic, that
only their ministers may officiate at the Lord's Table,
and that to allow inter-Communion compromises the
" catholic " view of the Church and its ministry.

A book, entitled *The Apostolic Ministry,* appeared
in 1946, edited by the Bishop of Oxford, in which in
scholarly fashion the " catholic " view of the Church
and its ministry is set forth in a notable series of es-
says. The book is written with historic erudition and
has been hailed by Anglo-Catholics as fully vindicat-
ing their exclusive views, which unchurch the vast
majority of Protestant Christians and deny the authority of the ministries in the communions to which they
belong. Professor T. W. Manson, well known and
honored for his valuable contributions to New Testament study, has taken up this question from the " evangelical " point of view, and in the following chapters
presents it with a painstaking treatment of the historical evidence, and above all with an insistence upon
the underlying Gospel of God.

For underneath the discussion of historical points lies a difference in the conception of God. The " catholic " view of the Church and its ministry assumes a legalistic idea of God, as One supremely concerned with the maintenance of a prescribed official structure of his Church, and limiting his present activities for the salvation of mankind and the edification of his Church to those who are " regular " in their adherence to the forms of its official structure. If he works outside of this structure and through other than the regularly ordained " successors " of the original apostles, it is of his overflowing kindness. Such ministries can only be incidental: they are not the apostolic ministry of the Church. But is such a legalistic doctrine of God compatible with his self-revelation in Christ? Is it the doctrine of God taught by Jesus or by Paul? Can one conceive of the Father of our Lord Jesus Christ with so fussy a concern for regularity in official posts and procedures? " Where the Spirit of the Lord is, there is liberty." The Church is an institution and must carry on its affairs in an orderly manner; but its essence is not i. the fixity of its official structure; it is in the continuing Spirit of Christ, ruling its life and work, and adapting them to varying circumstances in an ever changing world. Loisy wrote a generation ago:

" Great social institutions are governed by routine. . . . [But] immutability is merely apparent and fictitious, because institutions only endure by adapting themselves to the changing conditions of humanity."

Dr. Manson believes in the presence of the living
Christ in his Church. He rules it through orderly
processes, but he may do many things that to men
appear surprising and unprecedented. A ministry is
not apostolic merely because it can claim a traditional
pedigree going back directly to apostles. God is able
of stones to raise up children unto Abraham, and often
has raised up apostolic ministers without any claim
to a historical succession. " By their fruits ye shall
know them." A present and active Christ in his
Church is always at work and bestowing gifts. The
Church must have spiritual discernment to recognize
these gifts — in new interpretations of ancient con-
victions, in men and women endowed with qualities
of leadership, et cetera. There is no reason to dis-
parage time-honored offices — bishops, presbyters,
deacons, and many more. Their functions cannot help
varying in a world that does not remain the same in
successive centuries or in different lands. No evangelical Christian wishes to deny the spiritual ministry
exercised by many a Roman or Greek or Anglican
" catholic " bishop or priest or layman. It was note-
worthy that at Oxford in 1937, when *ᷨ.e Archbishop
of Canterbury invited the members of that ecumenical
conference to a service of Holy Communion in St.
Mary's, Methodist, Congregational, Presbyterian, and
other evangelicals attended and partook of the Supper
of the Lord. But the difficulty lies in the exclusiveness
of those who hold the " catholic " view. When the
Lord's Table was spread in the Dutch Reformed
Church in Amsterdam, and a similar invitation given
to all present at the World Council, few of those who

stand for the " catholic " position attended, or, if they were present, partook of the bread and cup.

Dr. Manson's book, with its clear and cogent setting forth of the " evangelical " view of the Church and its ministry, may serve to show that there is a conception as historically justified as the " catholic " conception represented in the book of the Bishop of Oxford and his colleagues. The " catholics " have their contribution to make to the more inclusive Church of God's tomorrow. But it cannot be made, so long as the exclusive features of that conception are retained. The " evangelical " view may need " catholic " amplification; but it conserves basic elements of the Gospel of God in Christ, which the Church cannot afford to lose.

HENRY SLOANE COFFIN.

AUTHOR'S NOTE

It is my earnest hope that this book may do something to make Christian people of all denominations more keenly aware of their real unity in the Body of Christ, a unity which our so-called "unhappy divisions" may obscure but cannot destroy.

T. W. M.

Manchester,
 May, 1948.

THE CHURCH

My reason for offering a few reflections on this topic is that its great importance has recently been recognized and emphasized in the learned and enthusiastic account of the apostolic ministry put together by a team of distinguished scholars under the leadership of the Bishop of Oxford. In some quarters the publication of this big and important work has given rise to jubilations which are, I venture to think, a little premature. There is a certain tendency to think that the last word has now been spoken; and that all that remains to do is to sit back and wait for the logical sequel in a reunited Church, a Church united on the only possible basis — the apostolic ministry as here set forth. Whether such reunion is possible on any other terms than submission of nonepiscopal communions to the episcopate, I need not try to determine; for I think it may be assumed that, in any case, such mass submissions are not likely to happen.

Moreover, it is not so certain that the question is settled. With the greatest respect for the scholarship and devotion of Dr. Kirk's team, one may feel doubts about the absolute finality of their conclusions. I cannot hope in the time at our disposal to attempt a detailed examination of the whole work, or even of the first five chapters, in which the crucial issues in the matter are discussed. I must be content to concentrate on a few points which seem to me to be vital. I shall group them under three main heads: the Church, the Apostolate, and the Settled Ministry.

THE CHURCH

My most vivid recollection of the Faith and Order Conference at Edinburgh in 1937 is that it began with a strong appeal by Archbishop Temple from the chair for concentration on the business of framing an adequate doctrine of the Church, the idea being that, if that were done, the problems connected with ministry and sacraments would be brought some way toward a solution. That appeal was not successful. The section of the Conference concerned with such matters as ministry and sacraments settled down instead to the discussion of formulas prepared by a committee presided over by the then Bishop of Gloucester. It speedily became apparent that any prima-facie attractiveness, which these propositions may have had, rested largely on ambiguities in statement; and as soon as the ambiguous terms were defined discord entered in. Along this road there was no prospect of agreement; and in fact no agreement was reached. Whether things would have gone better if Dr. Temple's way had been preferred to Dr. Headlam's it is not possible to say. What can be said is that it did offer a chance of progress, while the other carried with it the certainty of frustration.

I think that the work of the Bishop of Oxford and his colleagues is open to the same criticism, and this notwithstanding the fact that a whole chapter is devoted to the discussion by Dr. Thornton of the topic " The Body of Christ in the New Testament." For the treatment is open to serious objections. Dr. Thornton, rightly I think, insists on the necessity of understanding the thought of the New Testament writers regarding the Body of Christ in the light of their use of the Old Testament. We must " retrace their thoughts, reading the Old Testament as they read it. We must endeavor to see the scriptures *through their eyes* " (p. 54). But while this a perfectly right and proper procedure for the purpose of understanding how the minds of the New Testament writers worked, it does not follow that we are to be bound by their excursions into the more fanciful realms of rabbinical exegesis, much less by the wordplays and other haggadic fantasies which Dr. Thornton produces on his own account. Galatians 4:21–31 may furnish precious evidence about the way in which Paul's mind worked and the way in which its workings had been affected by his training in the school of Gamaliel. But we do not take the argument about Hagar and Sinai seriously. We do not regard it as proof of anything. At best it may be taken as an illustration of something else, and a poor illustration at that; for the thing it is supposed to illuminate is a good deal clearer without it.

It is true that we have to see the Old Testament as the New Testament writers saw it. And we have to make the necessary allowances. But the appeal to proof texts and the forced exegesis of words and phrases in the Old Testament text is not the main thing. It is not the fundamental and essential link between the Old Testament and the New. The real connection lies in the fact that the Old Testament presents us with a formulation of the purpose of God which becomes clearer and more definite as a result of successive divine revelations illuminating successive phases in the history of Israel. This divine purpose achieved its complete formulation in the mind of Jesus Christ and its complete realization in his life, death, and resurrection. The New Testament writers were well aware of it in its broad outlines, and were well able to state it, even though they could not always resist the temptation to add a few embellishments of rabbinical exegesis. We do less than justice to them and their message when we concentrate on the embellishments and forget the central core of the exposition.

For example, The Epistle to the Hebrews contains a good many examples of detailed exegesis of Old Testament texts, not all of which would appear equally convincing to modern scholars. But the same document contains one of the finest and clearest statements of the general principle in its opening verses.

" God, who in many and varied ways had spoken to our fathers in the past by the prophets, has spoken

to us in these last days by the son, whom he appointed the heir of all things, through whom also
he created the world. And he, who is the effulgence
of the divine glory and the perfect expression of the
divine nature, who, moreover, sustains the universe
by his word of power, he, when he had made puri-
fication for sins took his seat on the right hand of
the supreme Majesty, having become as much
superior to the angels, as the name he has inherited
is more excellent that theirs " (Heb. 1:1–4).

And, more than that, it contains in chs. 5 to 10 a
single sustained argument showing how God's purpose
that man should enter into perfect communion with
himself is one that goes back to the very beginnings of
Hebrew history, to the days of Abraham, for its first
proclamation how the whole apparatus of the Levitical priesthood and liturgy was nothing more than an
interim and ersatz dispensation, recognizing spiritual
needs which it could never fully satisfy and foreshad-
owing the coming of the perfect High Priest with his
perfect liturgy, whereby the divine purpose is realized.
This great argument makes it abundantly clear that
Christians are living in a liturgical new age. With
the advent of the perfect High Priest the Levitical
ordinances are surpassed and superseded. It is therefore no advance but a retrogression of the worst kind,
when the writer of I Clement, who was evidently familiar with the text of Hebrews, turns his back on its
central argument in order to buttress his own argu-

ments about the Church's ministry by an appeal to the ceremonial laws of the Old Testament.[1]

What is true of Hebrews is true of the other major documents of the New Testament. In the Pauline and Johannine writings we have, from other points of view, an equally clear insight into the essential purport of God's revelation from its first promise to its glorious fulfillment in Christ. And when we turn from these interpretations back to that which they interpret — the fact of Christ — we find all that the loftiest inspiration of the prophets and psalmists had suggested, all that the keenest insight of apostles and evangelists had understood, all this and more, embodied in the thought and action of Jesus. If we are to have an adequate conception of the ministry, it must be based on an adequate conception of the Church; and for that we must go to the Old Testament, not as a quarry for proof texts to be subjected to rabbinical exegesis, but as it is summed up and fulfilled in the mind and work of the Son of Man.

The Old Testament is the record, over something like a millennium and a half, of the relations between God and Israel, between God and one particlar people, with whom he had entered into a covenant, so that in a special and unique way he was their God and they were his people. This covenant made at the time of the Exodus was linked up to a still earlier promise

[1] Cf. Harnack, *Einführung in die alte Kirchengeshichte*, 93; E. Schweizer, *Das Leben des Herrn in der Gemeinde und ihren Diensten*, 131.

made to Abraham. The Sinai covenant was broken by Israel; and the Prophet Jeremiah has the promise of a new covenant written on the hearts of men. This new covenant is brought into being by Jesus at the Last Supper. The thought of it plays its part in the theology of the New Testament, particularly in The Epistle to the Hebrews. The Church is the new Israel, the people of God's new covenant.

But the new Israel is very far from being coextensive with the old. The significant history of Israel is the history of the Remnant, that is, the history of the minority in Israel who remain loyal to the covenant and to their covenant God. This Remnant, always there even when unobserved by man, is manifested in times of religious crisis. The nature of the crisis determines the way in which it will show itself. In the days of Elijah, when the living issue is that between Baalism and Yahwism, the Remnant is the seven thousand in Israel that have not bowed the knee to Baal. In the days of Isaiah and the Assyrian menace it is the company of people who accept the prophet's message, turn to God, and wait for his deliverance. Toward the end of the Exile the figure of the Servant of Yahweh in Deutero-Isaiah presents a conception of the Remnant not merely loyal to God or trusting in God, but also so completely dedicated to God that it can be the agent for the working out of his good purposes in the world. It is now a body whose service and sacrifice have a creative and constructive part to play in the affairs of God's Kingdom. In the days of Antiochus

Epiphanes, when the very existence of Israel's religion was threatened, and militant paganism was installed on Zion, The Book of Daniel sets over against the brute symbols of the heathen empires the manlike figure that represents " the people of the saints of the Most High." This idea of the Remnant plays its part in the Gospel story. Jesus gathers round himself a company of people who should embody the Remnant ideal as he sees it. They are called by him to share his knowledge of God and his service of the Kingdom alike in the exercise of its beneficent powers and in the sacrifices that must be made for it. And it is to be noted that they are not invited to create the Remnant, but to join it; not to build or bring the Kingdom of God, but to receive it and enter it.

This last point is of vital importance for the New Testament doctrine of the Church. It is of the essence of the matter that, while the Kingdom of God is not created by human effort, it *is* manifested in and through human lives. The manifestation is supreme and perfect in the Person and life of Jesus, insomuch that we can say, as Origen did, that he *is* the Kingdom. In the disciples of Jesus the manifestation is derivative and less than perfect, but still real and true. For our understanding of the nature of the Church it is necessary to know the ways in which the manifestation of the Kingdom takes place in the ministry of our Lord.

The word " ministry " gives the clue. For it is no accident that it is this word on which we have fixed to describe the public career of the Christ. It has a threefold fitness: (1) it reflects the fact that in Jesus we have the actualization of the purest and most perfect formulation of the Remnant ideal in the Old Testament, the picture of the Servant of the Lord in Deutero-Isaiah; (2) it accurately describes the kind of activities that make up the Gospel record; and (3) it provides the standard and pattern for the life of the followers of Jesus.

(1) It is characteristic of kingship as understood in the Old Testament that there is a king and that all others are his servants. The same word *'ebed* may stand for one of the great officers of state or for one of the palace servants. It applies equally to the free citizen and the slave. In relation to the king everyone from the least to the greatest is *'ebed,* servant. And what is true of the earthly kingdom is no less true of the heavenly. God is King and all men are his servants. Those who are of the Remnant are his willing servants. They offer themselves freely and without reserve. The picture of the Servant of the Lord in Isa., chs. 40 to 55, is a portrayal of what happens when the sovereignty of God is taken with complete seriousness in the world as it is.

(2) The ministry is just that picture come to life. What is presented to us in the Gospels is an increasingly high tension between Christ's version of the Kingdom and the Messiah and that of the rest of his contemporaries, including both his enemies and his friends. This tension emerges clearly in the tempta-

tions, which are best understood as an invitation to
Jesus to play the part of Messiah in a way that would
answer to Jewish expectations and Gentile appre-
hensions. He rejects the invitation. It comes again at
the time of Peter's confession at Caesarea Philippi,
and is as decisively rejected (Matt. 4:10; Mark 8:33).
The triumphal entry and the anointing at Bethany
may both be construed as attempts to make Jesus into
the kind of Messiah that was expected. Against all
this — and more of the same sort — Jesus maintained
his own conception of the Kingdom and the Messiah.
It depends on taking the Kingdom of God seriously
and saying, " In the Kingdom of God, God is King;
and all others, the Messiah included, are his servants."
The Messiah, indeed, must be the servant par excel-
lence: He must be *the* Servant of the Lord. It follows
at once that the Messianic career cannot be anything
but a ministry. Further, since the divine King is also
the heavenly Father, the Messianic ministry must be
a ministry that comes to help the helpless, to release
the captives, to seek and to save the lost. From first
to last that is what the ministry recorded in the Gospels
is. It is the constant, unwearied giving of divine service to men in body, mind, and spirit. This career
of self-giving has its culmination when the Servant
of the Lord, the Son of Man, gives his life a ransom
for many, lays down his life for his friends. We
grossly misunderstand the Gospel if we suppose that
in all this we are dealing with an interim dispensation,
a prelude to the coming of the Kingdom. This *is* the

Kingdom. The ministry of Jesus *is* the Kingdom of God spelled out in human terms.

(3) This perfect manifestation of the Kingdom at once becomes the norm for the life of Christ's followers. It is at this point that the typically Hebrew way of thinking about the individual and the social groups to which he belongs becomes important. It is well known that there is in Semitic thought the conception of what is called " corporate personality." It is commonplace that the members of a tribe or family can and do feel their unity with a vividness and concreteness strange to us. So Saint Paul can speak (Rom. 11:14) of " provoking his flesh " when he means provoking his fellow countrymen. This goes with the fact brought out clearly by Professor Johnson,[2] that among the Hebrews " a man's personality was thought of as extending throughout his ' household '; and that, indeed, the conception of the individual may not be dissociated from that of his kin-group (conceived in ever-widening circles of relationship) — with a resultant oscillation in thought as between the individual, the kin-group conceived as an association of individuals, and the kin-group thought of in vivid fashion as a single unit or corporate personality." Now this oscillation of thought is already apparent in the case of the Servant of the Lord in Isa., chs. 40 to 55. There has been endless discussion of the question whether the Servant is an

[2] A. R. Johnson, *The One and the Many in the Israelite Conception of God*, 25.

individual or a community; and texts can be quoted
to support either view. Similarly there is the fact that
in Daniel the term " Son of Man " is explicitly stated
to mean " the people of the saints of the Most High ";
that in the Gospels the sayings about the Son of Man
can be interpreted communally or individually; and
that in the event the destiny predicted by Jesus for
the Son of Man was fulfilled in his own person. There
is the further fact that Jesus began the creation of a
community of which he himself was the head and
center. By the time we come to the letters of Paul this
community, by now greatly enlarged, is thought of
as the " Body of Christ." In a word, the doctrine of
the Church is a branch of Christology. But this great
truth must be interpreted along the lines laid down
for us by Jesus. We may say, if we will, that the
Church is the continuation of the Incarnation; but this,
though true, is more awe-inspiring than illuminating.
For the Incarnation is a great mystery; and to say
that the Church is a continuation of the Incarnation
is simply to say that the Church is a great mystery.
It is, I venture to think, more profitable to begin more
modestly and say that the life of the Church is the
continuation of the Messianic ministry.

If we take this line, we must guard at the outset
against one grave error. We must not suppose that
" the continuation of the Messianic ministry " merely
means that certain admirable lines of conduct were
taught and practiced by the Great Prophet of Nazareth
who was martyred in the thirties of the first century;

and that other men of good will, convinced by his teaching and inspired by his example, have since been doing their best to follow in his footsteps. The " continuation of the Messianic ministry " means its continuation *by the Messiah*. The Body of Christ is the organism that he uses to carry out his purposes in the world in the same way that he used his physical body in the days of the ministry in Galilee and Judea. The essence of this way of thinking is that it most firmly believes and asserts the real presence of Christ in the Christian community. Consequently, when Dr. Kirk says that " our Lord endowed his Church with two great gifts: the means of grace (the word and the sacraments), and the ministry of grace (the apostles and their fellow-labourers)," [3] my complaint is not that this doctrine is too high, but that it is not high enough. Our Lord did better than that: he gave the Church himself. His real and abiding presence in the Church is the supreme " means of grace " and the supreme " ministry of grace." Other means of grace there are; but they are derivative and subordinate. Other ministries of grace there are; but they are one and all dependent on this.

This is the answer in principle to the distinction between the " essential " ministry and the " dependent " ministry, which plays so large a part in the argument of Dr. Kirk and his colleagues. There is one " essential " ministry, the only ministry that is unchallengeably essential. That is the ministry that

[3] *The Apostolic Ministry*, 8.

the Lord Jesus Christ opened in Galilee after John
the Baptist had been put in prison, the ministry that
he carried on in Galilee and Judea, the ministry that
he continues to this day in and through the Church,
which is his Body. The promise of this abiding presence, and its fulfillment in the Early Church, is as well
attested as anything in the New Testament.[4] It is in

[4] See Matt. 18:20. Here I am inclined to take the negative
form of the text as presented in D Syr[sin] and presupposed
in Clem. Al. as the original. So Wellhausen, Klostermann,
and Burkitt. ("You don't have two or three assembled in
my name without also having my presence with them.")
With this we may compare the saying of Hananiah b. Tera-
dion (*Aboth* iii. 3) that where there are two persons sitting
and occupying themselves with study of the Torah, the
Shekinah is between them. This goes with the Jewish view
that the presence of God is realized, not in a sacred building
but in the congregation assembled there. Cf. Schlatter, *Die
Theologie des Judentums nach dem Bericht des Josefus,*
73 f.; *Der Evangelist Matthäus,* 557 f. Cullmann suggests
that what is chiefly contemplated in this promise is the
realized presence of the Lord at the Eucharistic meal (cf.
Acts 1:3 f.; 10:41; Rev. 3:20) : *Urchristentum und Gottesdienst,* 12 f.; *La Signification de la Sainte-Cène dans le
Christianisme Primitif,* 4–15. See also W. Vischer, *Die
evangelische Gemeindeordnung,* 71 ff.

Matt. 28:20. On this, see Cullmann, *Christus und die Zeit,*
138–147, esp. 143; K. Holl, *Gesammelte Aufsätze,* ii. 53. The
abiding presence in the period from the Resurrection to the
Parousia is promised in connection with the missionary task
laid upon the Church by the risen Lord.

John 14:16–26. Here the promise is equally explicit. It
is closely connected with the promise of the Paraclete.

For the fulfillment in the experience of the first generation of Christians see Acts 18:10; II Tim. 4:16 f.

virtue of this presence that it is possible to call the Church the Body of Christ.[5]

The study of the ways in which the Church is described in the New Testament, and particularly the bringing together of the idea of the Body of Christ and the idea of " corporate personality," provides, I think, the clue to the solution of the ecclesiological puzzle propounded by the authors of the pamphlet *Catholicity,* whether the right order of things is: " Christ — faithful individuals — the Church " or " Christ — the Church — faithful individuals " (p. 13); alternatively expressed (p. 27) " Christ — the individual Christian — the Church " or " Christ — the visible Church — the individual Christian." As against any idea that the Church is constituted by a

---

[5] Here it should be mentioned that the Body of Christ is not the only designation of the Church in the New Testament. The other designations have been studied and classified in five groups in an important article by Professor de Zwaan in *Nederlandsch Theologisch Tijdschrift* i. 15–26. Broadly speaking we may recognize the figures of (1) Israel, people, nation, city, etc., where the individual is a citizen; (2) priesthood, temple, building, etc., where the individual is built into the structure — " edification "; (3) body, vine, olive, etc., where the individual is part of an organic whole, sharing in a life diffused through the whole; (4) election, adoption, and the like, where the individual is primarily the recipient of the unearned and undeserved grace of God; (5) virgin, bride, etc., where the idea of the individual is for the moment eclipsed by the idea of the Church as a " corporate personality." The whole paper deserves careful study.

number of persons, who agree with, say, the Sermon on the Mount, getting together and saying, " Let's form a Church," the authors of the pamphlet have every right to insist that Christ is not awaiting the approval or aid of any in order to have his Church. But that is not the whole of the matter. If it is true that the Church is not organized into existence by groups of believers, it is equally true that believers are not manufactured by the Church. The Church can create the environment favorable to the growth of Christians; it can bring spiritual influence to bear on people inside and out; but in the last resort the decision by which an individual becomes a disciple of Christ and a child of God is a private and personal affair between Christ and himself. It has always been so ever since Jesus first said, " Follow me." The Church is prior to any particular member; but equally that member's personal decision is prior to his Church membership. Salvation by faith and salvation by incorporation into the Body of Christ are not rival methods to be played off against one another: they are essential factors in any normal Christian experience.

The Church is the Body of Christ; and the life of the Church is the continuation of the Messianic ministry. It follows that the nature of the Church's task can be defined by reference to the records of the public career of Jesus, his teaching and his acts. Here we are given a clear lead. The Son of Man came not to be ministered to but to minister, and to give his

life a ransom for many. In other words the Son of
Man is the Servant of the Lord.[6] But if the Messianic
career has to be worked out in terms of service and
sacrifice, the followers of the Messiah must find their
destiny along the same lines. Every function of the
members of Christ's Body is a *diakonia* [service],
and Christ himself is the primary holder of every
diakonia.[7] The spirit and manner of this *diakonia* are
given by both precept and example. Jesus contrasts
the society which he has come to create with existing
societies, both Jewish and Gentile.

" You know that those who are recognized as
rulers of the gentiles lord it over them, and their
great ones exercise authority over them; but it is
not so among you. On the contrary, whoever is set
on becoming a great one among you shall be your
servant; and whoever is set on becoming your chief
shall be the slave of all " — (Mark 10:42 ff.).

" They [the Scribes and Pharisees] love the
places of honour at banquets and the seats of honour in the synagogues, and salutes in the market-
place and to be addressed by men as ' Rabbi.'
But don't you get the title ' Rabbi '; for one is your
teacher, and you are all brethren. And don't use

[6] See the very important observations in W. Manson's
Jesus the Messiah, 110 ff.

[7] E. Schweizer, *op. cit.*, 21 ff., 34–38, especially 32:
" *Es gibt nämlich im N.T. kaum eine Dienstbezeichnung,
die nicht auch als Bezeichnung des Christus selbst vorkäme.*"

the title ' Father ' on earth[8]; for one is your Father, he who is in heaven. And don't get the title of ' Instructor ' either; for one is your Instructor, the Messiah. And your greatest one shall be your servant [*diakonos*] " — (Matt. 23:6–11).

When the disciples are sent out on their own, their instructions are about the service they are to render. The intention of Jesus when he appointed the Twelve was that he should " send them out to proclaim [the Kingdom of God] and to have power to expel demons," i.e., to bring help to those who were afflicted in body, mind, or spirit by the powers of evil (Mark 3:14 f.). This intention becomes the marching orders of the Twelve (Mark 6:7–11) ; and the Evangelist records that these instructions were duly carried out. The Twelve preached, expelled demons, and successfully treated cases of sickness by anointing (Mark 6:12 f.). This account is confirmed by the evidence furnished by the other Gospels, whether we regard it as parallel accounts of the one mission of the Twelve or independent description of a different mission sent out on another occasion.The disciples are sent out as laborers in the harvest fields or as lambs among wolves (Luke 10:2 f.; Matt. 9:37 f.; 10:16, Q.). They justify their existence and earn their keep by the service they render (Luke 10:7; Matt. 10:10, Q.).

[8] In this verse I read υμιν with D Θ *l*26 Lat Syr[vet] pesh. Cf. Joüon, *L'Evangile de notre Seigneur Jésus-Christ*, 140.

There is what appears to be another formulation of the instructions in Matt. 10:5–8. I quote verses 7, 8:

"And as you travel along make the proclamation that the Kingdom of Heaven has drawn near. Heal the sick, raise the dead, cleanse the lepers, expel the demons. Freely you have received, freely give."

Luke 10:17–20 gives an account of the disciples' report on their return from the mission, which tells the same story as the others. It is important to be clear about all this teaching and its practical application. When Jesus says, " He that would be great shall be a servant," he does not mean that the overambitious will be punished by being reduced to menial jobs. Nor does he mean that those who want promotion can earn it by doing some menial jobs first. On the contrary, just as the ministry of the Messiah is the manifestation of the Kingdom of God, so the ministry of the disciple is the manifestation of the greatness he seeks. In the Kingdom of God service is not a stepping-stone to nobility: it *is* nobility, the only kind of nobility that is recognized.

This conception of the nature of the Christian community's task is not confined to the period of the earthly ministry, whether that of Jesus in person or in the extended form in which on occasion he entrusted it to his disciples. We have eloquent statements of the duty of the Church, and in particular of its leaders, in such passages as Paul's address to the

Ephesian elders at Miletus (Acts 20:18–35), or his account of the ministry in II Cor., chs. 3 to 7, or the exhortation in I Peter 5:1–5 — impressive in any case, and particularly so if it comes from the apostle himself — or the charge to Peter in John 21:15–17. Specially illuminating is the testimonial to the household of Stephanas in I Cor. 16:15 ff. They have two titles to honor: they are the first fruits of Achaia, and they have laid themselves out to be of service (*diakonia*) to the saints. In their service of the community they have manifested their fitness for leadership. It is perhaps not necessary to multiply instances.

What does all this amount to? If the preceding discussion is sound, we are in a position to say something about the Church that our Lord launched upon the world. And what we have to say is remarkably in accord with the closing words of Saint Matthew's Gospel. The Church, represented by the Eleven, is given a task of evangelization and education, that is, a work involving both missionary propaganda among the unconverted and training and discipline of those within the community. It is given a norm or pattern for its work. This is implied in the fact that they are to make disciples, and that what they are to teach the disciples is what they themselves, as disciples, have been commanded by Jesus. It is given the abiding presence of Christ, who holds all the power needed for the fulfillment of the task. The outstanding point here is that the Church is at one and the same time the dwelling place of the living Christ and the guardian of the tradition set up by the Messianic ministry. It is at once the Body of the exalted Christ and the Body of the humiliated Christ; it shares the existence of the crucified and the risen Christ. Its afflictions, in its members serve to fill up what is lacking to the sufferings of Christ.[9] At the same time through the gift of the Spirit it shares the risen life of its Lord. These things can be distinguished in thought: they cannot be separated in fact. They are essential, inseparable aspects of the life of the Body of Christ. To separate them is to open the way to erroneous views about the nature of the Church.

The sort of error that arises from stressing either of these facts at the expense of the other is well brought out by Professor Eduard Schweizer in his book to which I have already referred, *Das Leber des Herrn in der Gemeinde und ihren Diensten*, Ch. III, §§ 18–20 (pp. 107–134). He rightly points out that overemphasis on the possession of the Spirit and on sharing the risen life of Christ can lead, and does lead, only too easily to a gnostic Christianity, to the religion enjoyed by a spiritual upper ten, who imagine that they can be at ease in Zion, and live as *rentiers* on the income of their gilt-edged securities in heaven. They are irked by the fact that the Church has to live in this world and carry on here the ministry of the humiliated and crucified Christ. It seems to be an

---

[9] Col. 1:24. Cf. Rom. 8:17; Gal. 6:17; Rom. 6:3 ff. See Cullmann, *Königsherrschaft Christi und Kirche im N.T.*, 30 f.

invasion of the glorious liberty of the children of God. On the other side overemphasis of the conception of the continuing ministry can, and does, lead to increasing emphasis on the institutional aspects of the Church's life, with more and more organization and more and more demand for obedience to constituted authority. The danger is that not only the individual Christian, but even Christ himself, will be forbidden to do anything except through the proper channels. The Body of Christ is mechanized.

But when the post-Resurrection Church began its work at Pentecost, two factors were present: (1) the apostles as representing the ministry of Christ who had taken the form of a servant and become obedient unto death, even the death of the cross. They had been his companions in the ministry and the witnesses of his Passion.[10] (2) The Holy Spirit, the Paraclete promised by Christ and now given. Both alike are " sent " by Christ. In other words Christ is prior — logically and temporally — to apostles *and* to the Paraclete; and it is as we realize that priority as the absolute primacy of Christ in his Church that the genuine unification of the two aspects of the Church's life takes place, and we see a ministry whose norm is the ministry of Jesus — servant of all; servile to none — and a liberty of the Spirit that does not degenerate into license.

This means that we take the organic conception

[10] This is true whether or not any of them had been physically present at the Crucifixion.

of the Church in deadly earnest. When we do that, we find only one essential and constitutive ministry, that of the Head, our Lord Jesus Christ. All others are dependent, derivative, functional. From this point of view we can all heartily agree with Dr. Kirk in his protests against regarding the bishop as a cog in the diocesan machine. Things are very far wrong when any member of the Body of Christ has become a cog in a machine. But while cog-in-a-machine is too low a status for any Christian, member of the Body of Christ, partaker of his Spirit, and sharer of his ministry is not too high for any. In any case there is none higher.

THE APOSTOLATE

In the last lecture it was argued that we must understand the nature of the ministry in the light of the nature of the Church; and that the nature of the Church can only be adequately understood in the light of the Old Testament conception of the Remnant as perfectly realized in Jesus. That leads to the doctrine of the Church as the Body of Christ and of the Church's life as the continuation of the Messianic ministry. This continuing ministry is governed by the example laid down by Jesus in the thirties of the first century (here the apostles are pre-eminently the eye-witnesses and ministers of the word from the beginning — Luke 1:2); and by the promised presence of the Spirit of Christ in his community, recalling to mind and elucidating the things laid down by Jesus in his earthly ministry (cf. John 14:26). It has been urged that if we take the thought of the Church as the Body of Christ seriously, we must conclude that the only " essential ministry " in the Church is that involved in the continual presence of Christ himself, and that all others are derivative, dependent, and functional. " He [Christ] gave some to be apostles; and some, prophets; and some, evangelists; and some, pastors and teachers; for the perfecting of the saints, unto the work of ministering, unto the building up of the body of Christ " (Eph. 4:11 f.). All alike, from apostles to teachers, are objects of the same verb " gave," whose subject is Christ. All alike are organs of the one Body.

Now the Church is the embodiment of the Remnant ideal. It is a society within a society. But it is not an isolationist group, carefully fostering a private life of its own secluded from the contaminations of the world. It has to discharge a task in the world as well as to maintain its own inner life. It has to present the Gospel to those outside; and it can only do that effectively as its members live according to Christ in their relations to one another. In other words the Church has a dual role — apostolic in relation to those outside and pastoral in relation to those within. (It is a pity that the word " apostolic " has had its meaning narrowed in the course of the centuries, so that instead of declaring primarily the Church's commitment to a great missionary task, it merely registers a claim on the part of the Eastern and Roman communions to be the lawful successors of the apostles).[11] Both ministries serve the same purpose, the building up (*oikodome*) of the Body of Christ whether by bringing in new members or by making

[11] Loofs, *Symbolik,* i. 142 (the Orthodox Church); 221 (Roman Catholic).

better members of those already in. The apostolic task is one of proclaiming the good news (*kerygma*); the pastoral task is that of instruction in Christian truth and training in Christian worship (*didache*). These are not separate things: they are two aspects of a single life. Sometimes and in some cases one aspect is more prominent than another; but neither is absent in a healthy Church life.

One important consequence follows from these considerations. It is that if we would understand the Church of the New Testament and the early centuries, we must make full use of the experience of the mission field, and particularly of missionary work among idolatrous peoples. Some work has been done already; and it has not had anything like the attention it deserves. But much more could be done, and there is a great field of research wide open for anyone who can bring together the life of the Primitive Church as reflected in its documents and the life of the Churches of the mission field as it is known to those who are engaged in the work.[12] One thing is very clear from the information available, and that is the immense

[12] T. M. Lindsay showed the importance of this matter in his book *The Church and the Ministry in the Early Centuries*. Some splendid pioneer work was done by a scholarly missionary of the Presbyterian Church of England in Formosa, Dr. Campbell Moody, in his books, *The Heathen Heart* and *The Mind of the Early Converts*. Schweizer refers to an article by W. Freytag, " *Die gemeinde und ihre Ämter in der missionarischen Erfahrung* " (*Ev. Missionszeitschrift* 1942, 264–276).

importance of the missionary, not only in making the initial impact of the Gospel on a heathen community, but also in helping the Christian communities that come into existence to assimilate an adequate amount of sound Christian doctrine. It needs a long time to produce a mature settled ministry and a mature Church membership, starting from zero. In the light of what happens on the mission field we need not be surprised at the immense importance of the apostles in the Primitive Church: it is just what we should expect. For it is just in that situation that the need of apostolic guidance and help is greatest. It is true, and the New Testament is witness to the truth, that the individual Christian community may owe its existence, under God, to the apostle,[13] and not only its existence but also its continued spiritual health. But while the apostle is essential in this way to the local community, it does not follow that he is essential in the same way to the Church as a whole. The Church of Christ was there before Paul the apostle, though the Church at Corinth was not. It may be that apostleship is just one of the ways in which Christ continues his ministry in the Church, that apostleship is a function of the Church and the apostolate the organ through which it is exercised. If that be so, the Church is indeed apostolic, not merely in virtue of tracing its pedigree back to the apostles, but much more in virtue of doing the work of an apostle.

[13] Saint Paul makes precisely this claim in respect of the Corinthian community (I Cor. 4:14 f.).

The question, however, is not quite so simple as that. It is complicated by the fact that some of the men called apostles in the New Testament form a definite group standing in a special relation to Jesus himself. The Twelve had been chosen by our Lord and appointed to be his companions and, on occasion at least during the ministry, his representatives. It is clear from Saint Paul's letters that the Twelve were called apostles in the earliest days of the Palestinian Church. This means that the Hebrew and Aramaic equivalents of the Greek word *apostolos* are important for the ascertaining of the meaning of the term.[14]

The Hebrew term is *shaliach,* a derivative from the verb *shalach,* to send, which in the Septuagint is regularly rendered by *apostellein,* the verb corresponding to *apostolos.* Concerning the use of the verb in the Old Testament, Rengstorf says that the emphasis is on the sender rather than the person sent. This is in line with the fact noted by Professor Johnson[15] that a member of a man's household acting as his agent or messenger becomes, as it were, an ex-

---

[14] For the Jewish material, reference may be made to the article by K. H. Rengstorf in Kittel's *Theol. Wörterbuch zum N.T.*, i. 397–448; H. Vogelstein, in *Monats. f. Gesch. Wiss. Jud.*, 49 (1905), 427 ff. (this is not accessible to me), and *Hebrew Union College Annual*, 2 (1925), 99–123; S. Krauss, in *Encyclopædia Judaica* III. 1–10; Billerbeck, *Komm.* iii. 2–4; iv. 149–152; Juster, *Les Juifs dans l'Empire Romain,* i. 388 ff., 405.

[15] *Op. cit.,* 8 ff., citing Gen. 44:4 ff., Judg. 11:12 f.

tension of his master's personality, so that through the agency of the messenger the master may be regarded as being present in person. The messengers " as ' extensions ' of their master's personality, are treated as actually *being* and not merely representing their lord " (p. 10).

The noun *shaliach* has a variety of uses. The present discussion will follow in the main the classification adopted by Rengstorf.

(1) We have the *shaliach* as messenger or agent of an individual. This is the arrangement common in all organized communities whereby a person may delegate to another the power to do on his behalf something which he is entitled to do for himself but finds it inconvenient or impossible to do in person. The principle laid down by the rabbis is that " a person's *shaliach* is like himself," that is, that within the terms of his commission the agent's actions count as those of his principal, and the rights of the principal are enforceable by the agent. We are dealing here in Jewish law with much the same kind of thing that is dealt with in Roman law under the general heading *de Mandato*.[16] There is one important point here, which must be discussed since it has a bearing on the doctrine of apostolic succession: that is the question whether a *shaliach* could transmit his commission to another. To this I think the answer is, " No."

[16] Jolowicz, *Historical Introd. to Roman Law*, 307 f.; Gaius, *Inst.* III. 155–162; Justinian, *Inst.* III. 26. Cf. the maxim of English law: *Qui facit per alium facit per se.*

In the Mishnah (*Gittin* iii. 6), the case is discussed of a divorce where the husband is abroad and sends the writ of divorce [17] by the hand of a *shaliach*. The *shaliach* falls sick and is unable to complete his mission. What is to be done? The answer of the Mishnah is that the court (*beth din*) appoints another person and sends him to serve the writ. The original *shaliach* must say in the presence of the court, " It (the writ) was written in my presence, and it was signed in my presence," thus authenticating the document to the court in the same terms in which he would have authenticated it to the wife, if he had been able to deliver it himself. Naturally the new messenger cannot say this; and the rule is that he must say instead, " I am the *shaliach* of the court." It seems clear that the first *shaliach,* when he finds himself unable to fulfill his commission, formally hands over the document to the court, which then appoints its own *shaliach* to serve the writ on *its* behalf. The new *shaliach* is the *shaliach* of the court. He is not the *shaliach* of the original *shaliach.*[18]

Another point to be borne in mind is that in the main the *shaliach* has a definite commission, that his authority does not extend beyond his terms of reference, and that it lapses when the commission has been executed. Here there is an illuminating piece of documentary evidence. We have in the Palestinian Tal-

[17] Cf. Deut. 24:1–4; Mark 10:1–12.
[18] Cf. the maxim in English law: *Delegatus non potest delegare.*

mud [19] a letter of commendation or authorization from the Patriarch R. Judah II in favor of R. Hiyya b. Abba, who was going abroad. The date is probably the last quarter of the third century A.D. The letter runs: "Behold we send to you a great man as our *shaliach;* and he is our representative [lit., equivalent to us] until such time as he returns to us." The authorization of the rabbi is for the duration of his stay abroad; as soon as the stay comes to an end, the authority lapses.[20]

In this connection we may consider the *apostoli* (*sheluchim*) of the Jewish patriarchs.[21] An important function of these officers was the collection on behalf of the patriarch of the sums of money collected in the Diaspora for the support of the rabbinate. This fund (the *migbath hakamim*) was raised locally by the synagogue officials and received by the *apostoli* sent by the patriarch.[22] These *apostoli* were usually chosen from the most eminent rabbis; and we are told that they were empowered to do much more than collect money. They had the supervision of the officers of the local Jewish communities. They could inspect

[19] p. *Hagigah* 76 d 3 f. Parallel in p. *Ned.* 42 b 22 f.
[20] For a discussion of this and other passages bearing on the limitations of delegated authority among the rabbis see Billerbeck, *Komm.* ii. 656 ff.
[21] On these see especially Juster, *op. cit.,* and Billerbeck, *Komm.* iii. 316 ff.
[22] C. Th. 16.8.14 (11 Ap. 399) quoted Juster i. 386 n.2: ". . . *quos ipsi apostolos uocant, qui ad exigendum aurum adque argentum a patriarcha certo tempore diriguntur.*"

the teaching of the law in the synagogues of the Dispersion and, if necessary, give teaching themselves by means of sermons in the synagogues.[23] Along with this goes the statement of Justin Martyr in his *Dialogue with Trypho* (§§ 17, 108, 117) that anti-Christian propaganda was carried on from Jerusalem as center by means of agents whom he describes as " picked men," " ordained " and " sent out all over the civilized world." At a later date Eusebius, commenting on Isa. 18:1,[24] refers to these missions, calls the messengers *apostoloi,* and informs us that in his day the bearers of encyclical letters from the rulers of the Jewish community were still called *apostoloi.* It is to be noted that Justin does not use the word *apostolos* for these representatives of the Jewish central authority; but this may only be because the word had peculiarly honorable associations in Christian circles. What is very important is the fact, pointed out by Rengstorf,[25] that all the functions discharged by the Jewish *apostoli* are functions *within the Jewish community.* They do not appear as the " foreign missionaries " of Judaism. The contrast with the Christian apostolate is very striking. Along with this goes the fact that the conversions to Judaism that took place in the early centuries of our era appear to be the

[23] Juster, *op. cit.,* i. 389.

[24] Text in Otto's note on *Dial,* § 17.

[25] *Op. cit.,* 418. Cf. Abrahams, *Studies in Pharisaism and the Gospels* ii. 69–71, who rightly insists on the strictly defensive character of the activities of the men referred to by Justin.

results of what might be called private enterprise
rather than official action.

(2) We have the *shaliach* as the representative of
a corporate body. Here there are two bodies mainly
concerned: the court (*beth din*) and the synagogue
congregation (*ṣibbur*), and the functions of the *shaliach* are accordingly legal and administrative or liturgical. The *shaliach* of the court has various functions:
for example, to serve a document authenticated by
the court, to collect money on behalf of the court, or
to convey the instructions of the court to someone. The
most striking example is the appointment of delegates
of the court to prepare the High Priest for the services
of the Day of Atonement, as described in the Mishnah
(*Yoma* i). Similar is the sending out of rabbis to
carry through the decisions of the sanhedrin regarding the Jewish calendar, especially in the matter of
intercalation.[26] We also hear of delegates deputed
to announce the beginning of the new month. All
these are administrative functions in the community.

We now turn to the *ṣheliach ṣibbur*, the representative of the synagogue in its corporate worship.[27] It

[26] Mishnah, *Yebamoth* xvi. 7 R. Akiba goes to Nehardea.
T. Megillah ii. 5 R. Meir goes to the province of Asia. The
decision to intercalate was intimated by letter. (We have a
specimen of such a letter sent out by R. Gamaliel II: text
in Dalman's *Aramäische Dialektproben*. It seems probable
that the delegate was the bearer of the letter and had the
task of carrying it into effect.
[27] See Billerbeck, *Komm.* iv. 149–152; Elbogen, *Der
Jüdische Gottesdienst*, 2, 487 ff.

was his task to lead the prayers of the congregation; and in the early synagogue the term did not designate an office but a function, which might be performed by any member of the synagogue who was able and willing.[28] Here the interesting question is what was the relation between the *ṣibbur* and the *shaliach*, between the congregation and its representative. The Mishnah transfers into this field the general rule that " a man's agent is like to himself." So in *Berakhoth* v. 5 we are told that if a man in saying his private prayers makes an error in the recitation of the *Tefillah*, it is a bad omen for him personally. If, however, he is saying the same prayers as *ṣheliach ṣibbur*, it is a bad omen for those who appointed him as their *shaliach*, because a man's agent is like to himself. That is, in leading the prayer the *shaliach* really represents the congregation.

The nature of this representation is raised by another Mishnah passage (*Rosh Hashshanah* iv. 9), which, in Danby's translation (*The Mishnah* 194), runs as follows: " Like as the agent of the congregation is bound [to say the daily *Tefillah*], so is each person bound. Rabban Gamaliel says: The agent of the congregation fulfills the obligation that rests upon the many." Here the essential point is that the daily

---

[28] At a later time the increasing complexity and elaboration of the Jewish liturgy led to the appointment of regular ministers for this service; but for the early days Elbogen's statement is that *ṣheliach ṣibbur* " *nicht ein ständiges Amt bezeichnet, sondern nur die Tätigkeit, der er im Augenblick obliegt* " (p. 488).

recitation of the *Tefillah* is an obligation on all Is-
raelites (*Ber.* iii. 3). The question is whether that
obligation can be fulfilled by proxy. The decision,
Rabban Gamaliel dissenting, is that it cannot.[29] This
raises the deeper problem whether in worship anyone
can deputize for anyone else. One person may cer-
tainly pray (by way of intercession) for another; but
can one person say another's prayers for him? This
question is bound up with another, which also arises
in the Talmud in connection with the Temple ritual.
In *Ķiddushin* 23 b. (Billerbeck, iii. 4), Rab Huna b.
Joshua (*c.* A.D. 350) argues that an agent can do for
his principal only what the principal is entitled to do
for himself. But the ordinary Israelite is not entitled
to perform the sacrificial ritual. Therefore the priests,
when they officiate in the Temple, do so not as agents
of the worshiping people but as *sheliché de Rachmana,*
agents of the Merciful One. It comes to this that the
shaliach of the synagogue congregation is only a use-
ful functionary for the purposes of corporate and
public worship. He does nothing that the individual
worshiper is not able and obliged to do for himself.
He is the voice of the congregation, through whom
all speak. It is otherwise with the priest, according
to Rab Huna. He does something which the congregation cannot do. Therefore he cannot be their *shaliach.* Therefore he must be God's. But this is the *re-
ductio ad absurdum* of the idea of a priestly caste.

[29] For this text and the Talmudic discussion arising out
of it, see Billerbeck, *Komm.* iv. 151.

Such a caste, once it is credited with the possession of *exclusive* powers, ceases to be representative of the worshipers. So we come to the strange conclusion that God has to offer sacrifices to himself by the hands of his agents the priests. The moral is sufficiently obvious.

(3) We have the *shaliach* as God's agent. We have already dealt with the case in which the priest in the Temple is conceived as the representative of the Merciful One. One would have thought that, even more than the priests, the prophets would have been brought into this category, especially in view of such passages as the inaugural vision of Isaiah, with its divine call (Isa. 6:8), " Whom shall I send, and who will go for us? " Yet the fact is that the term *shaliach* is not normally applied to the prophets. There are four exceptions: Moses, Elijah, Elisha, and Ezekiel. But these four are not styled *shaliach* in virtue of their prophetic message, but in virtue of the performance of great miracles which ordinarily lie in the power of God alone. Such are the removal of barrenness (II Kings 4:16 f.) in the case of Elisha; the raising of the dead in the cases of Elijah (I Kings 17:21–23), Elisha (II Kings 4:34–36), and Ezekiel (Ezek., ch. 37); and the bringing of rain in the case of Elijah (I Kings 17:1; 18:1). Here these men are thought of as God's *sheluchim*, in that they do on God's behalf things that lie in God's power and there alone.

What emerges from the consideration of the Jewish

evidence regarding the *shaliach?* First, that he performs on behalf of someone else, whether an individual or a corporate body, functions which his principal is himself entitled to perform. Secondly, that the
nature of his activities, and in some cases their duration, is defined, so that his authority does not go
beyond the terms of his commission. Thirdly, that
his commission is not transferable. When he ceases to
exercise it, the authority reverts to the principal.
Fourthly, that *shaliach* is not a term of status but of
function. Fifthly, that in so far as the *shaliach* has a
religious commission it is always exercised within
the borders of Jewry, and does not involve what we
should call missionary activity.

We must now ask how far the conception of the
shaliach in Judaism may have influenced the Christian conception of the apostle. In the first place it can
be said that the general idea is the same in both cases.
The *apostolos* in the New Testament, like the *shaliach*
in Judaism, is sent and commissioned by someone
for some purpose. Corresponding to the rabbinic
dictum that the *shaliach* is like his principal, we have
the statement (John 13:16) that " the servant is not
greater than his master, nor is the *apostolos* greater
than he that sent him." [30] As in Judaism so in Christianity, the *apostolos* can be the representative of a
community, as in II Cor. 8:23 and Phil. 2:25. In both
cases the " apostles " in question are charged with
the delivery of the gifts of the community to those in

[30] Rengstorf, *op. cit.*, 421 f.

need of them. But, of course, the main use of the term in the New Testament is in connection with the proclamation of the Gospel. Of the 79 examples of the word in the New Testament, 29 are in the Pauline Epistles (excluding the Pastorals) and 28 in The Acts. Here the primary application of the term is to the Twelve. Paul claims the title for himself consistently and acknowledges it in the case of James, the Lord's brother (Gal. 1:19). In Acts 14:4, 14, Paul and Barnabas are called apostles. In Rom. 16:7 the same title is given to Andronicus and Junias, two otherwise unknown Jewish Christians.[31] It is possible that in I Cor. 15:7 the appearance of the risen Lord " to all the apostles " indicates a larger group than the Twelve; though it may be, as Holl maintains, that the expression means no more than the Eleven plus James the Lord's brother. In any case the Twelve, with Paul and James the Just, stand by themselves. Equally, as Lightfoot pointed out,[32] if the number of the apostles had been definitely fixed, it would be impossible to account for the rise of the false apostles mentioned in II Cor. 11:13 and Rev. 2:2. It seems clear that we have to reckon with a stricter and a looser use of the term both in the New Testament and in the early Christian literature.

Starting from the fact that the Twelve are undis-

[31] This is the usual interpretation of the text. See Sanday and Headlam *in loc.*; Lightfoot, *Galatians,* 96 n.l. It is rejected by K. Holl, *Ges. Aufs.* ii. 47 f.

[32] *Galatians,* 97.

puted holders of the title of apostle in the New Testament, we must ask whether they were so called by Jesus. On this point we have the evidence of Mark 3:13 ff.: " And he went up into the hill-country and summoned the men of his choice; and they went off to join him. And he appointed twelve who were to be his companions and were to be sent out by him to preach and to have power to expel demons." Here we have a selection from a larger group of followers. Those so chosen are to be in close contact with Jesus, learning from him the ways of the Kingdom. That is the immediate intention. Later they are to be sent out with a definite commission from their Master to perform specific tasks. It is not implied that they will be sent out only on a single occasion. The language of Mark would allow a number of missions, and it may be accident that we are told of only one in Mark. We are informed by Matthew (ch. 10:5 f.) that the mission which is recorded was confined to Israel. Mark describes this mission in ch. 6:7–13 and the return from it in ch. 6:30. It is here that he calls the Twelve " apostles "; and it is clear that, if we see behind the Greek word the Aramaic equivalent, the correct word is being used to describe what is taking place. The Twelve are commissioned: they are given a definite task and the necessary power to fulfill it. Their appointment covers a limited period, at the end of which they return and report what they have done. Rengstorf finds in Mark 9:38–41 further evidence, indirect indeed but all the more impressive for that, of the apostolate of the Twelve during the ministry.[33]

When Mark tells us that Jesus gave the Twelve power to expel demons, we may compare the statement of Jesus himself (Luke 11:19 f.; Matt. 12:27 f., Q.), "If I by the finger of God cast out demons . . ." It comes to this, that the apostles act as the agents of Jesus in the same way that he acts as the agent of God.

On the formal side the relation between Jesus and the Twelve corresponds admirably to the relation between a principal and his *sheluchim* in Jewish usage. What is distinctive of the *shaliach* of Jesus is not the form of his commission but its content. Jesus has given to apostleship the same content that he had given to Messiahship, thus making it inevitable that those who would represent him must represent him in *his* way.

We have further to notice that the kind of commission described by Mark for the Twelve is not necessarily confined to them. The fact that Luke records a similar mission of a much larger number is evidence either that such a mission in fact took place; or that, if it did not, the idea of such a mission in other hands than those of the Twelve was not intolerable in the Primitive Church. During the ministry it would seem that apostleship was a function rather than a status. The Twelve were sent as the representatives of their Master; and so were others. The picture of the retinue

[33] *Op. cit.*, 426.

of Jesus during the ministry, as it emerges from the Gospels, is one of a series of concentric circles of people. The outer and largest contains those who were attracted by the teaching of Jesus or drawn to seek his help. Within this circle is another of those who actively respond to his call for repentance and belief in the good news. A still smaller group become followers in more or less close attendance on him. Within this circle of followers we find smaller groups like the Seventy (-two) and the Twelve. And even within the Twelve there is a smaller group of three who enjoy a special intimacy. But while there are these degrees of intimacy and of responsible sharing in the work of the ministry, there do not seem to be any permanent appointments during the course of the ministry.[34] Rengstorf points out, with justice, that

[34] It may be noted that the special treatment accorded to Peter, James, and John within the circle of the Twelve might well have raised hopes of special positions in their minds. We know that such hopes were in fact entertained by James and John (Mark 10:37). And here it may be remarked that this request of the sons of Zebedee implies that they are not aware of any special privileges accorded to anyone else. They could hardly have asked for first and second places if the first place was already assigned to Peter. Equally the statement of Peter himself at Mark 10:28 implies that no special mark of favor has been conferred on any member of the Twelve — not even Peter, who here identifies himself with the rest. This seems to mean that if Matt. 16: 17 ff. is a genuine word of Jesus, it can hardly be in place in its present context.

On the parity of the Twelve, cf. M. Barth, *Der Augenzeuge*, 27.

the behavior of the Twelve in the closing scenes of
the earthly ministry is an indication that they had
not been given permanent posts as lieutenants. They
had a promise, to which we return presently, of sitting
on twelve thrones and judging the twelve tribes of
Israel (Matt. 19:28; Luke 22:28–30). It required
the risen Christ to set them on their feet and give them
a new commission.

The starting point for the study of this new commission is the account of the Resurrection appearances
of the Lord given by Saint Paul at the beginning of
I Cor., ch. 15. Here he puts his own apostleship on a
par with that of the Twelve by setting his experience
on the Damascus Road alongside their experiences
of the risen Christ. Equally when he insists in Gal.
1:12 ff. that his Gospel is not from men but by revelation of Jesus Christ, he is claiming for himself what
could be claimed for the Twelve. In the post-Resurrection world it is not enough to have been a companion
of Jesus during the earthly ministry or even to have
been sent out by him on missions connected with it.
The death and resurrection of Christ have made a
vital difference to the men who are sent out and to the
content of their message.[35] This difference can be
summed up by saying that new power had been re-
leased. Pentecost is the proper sequel to the cross
and Resurrection; and the immediate result of Pentecost is new fervor, new courage, new confidence mani-

[35] On this, see P. Feine, *Paulus*, 219–224; K. Holl, *Ges.
Aufs.* ii. 52 ff.

fested in the conduct of the Twelve. At the same time a new and better understanding of the meaning and purpose of the ministry became possible. This understanding was embodied in the kerygma. It was now possible to see more clearly the implications of apostleship and to set about its tasks with greater courage and effectiveness than ever before. But the character of the ministry itself had not changed. Its pattern had been laid down once and for all by Jesus. The apostles had been the witnesses of the ministry. They were now in addition the witnesses of the Resurrection. This is the qualification for post-Resurrection apostleship, which Paul claims to share with the Twelve and with James the Just: to have seen the risen Lord and to have been commissioned by him. Paul apparently thought of himself as the last to receive this experience. He took the experience in deadly earnest; and as his Lord had laid down the pattern of apostleship in the ministry, so Paul sought to work it out in the first and most glorious foreign missionary enterprise of the Christian Church.

It is in the working out of apostleship that we get its ratification in what Saint Paul calls the " signs of the apostle," whether they be spectacular works of power or the less spectacular, but not less impressive, evidences furnished by changed lives and new communities living in the spirit and power of Christ. Paul claimed this ratification for his apostleship.

But while Paul claimed parity with the Twelve in the matter of apostleship, he did not claim to be one of the Twelve. Nor did anyone else. It was recognized that the Twelve stood in a unique position; and it is desirable that we should see clearly what that position was. We have already had before us some evidence that the Twelve formed a closed group during the ministry, and that quite late in the ministry Jesus was flatly refusing to countenance anything that would compromise the parity of the Twelve. It seems to me that this conception of the Twelve is clearly implied in the promise of the twelve thrones (Matt. 19:28; Luke 22:28–30). This promise should probably be regarded as coming late in the ministry, but before Jesus was aware of the treachery of Judas.[36] It has a marked eschatological reference, especially in the Matthaean version. The Twelve have the assurance of special places and special tasks at the Parousia. This promise is echoed in the constructive visions of the Apocalypse. The seer's vision of the New Jerusalem shows it provided with twelve gates, each assigned to one of the tribes of Israel. Corresponding to the twelve gates are the twelve foundations of the wall; and on these foundation stones are inscribed the twelve names of the twelve apostles of the Lamb. When it is recalled that the gate is the traditional courthouse of the Israelite city, it is not difficult to see in this feature of the New Jerusalem the fulfillment of the promise to the Twelve.

With this goes a very significant fact. In The Acts

[36] The position in Luke seems to me impossibly late.

we are given a full and circumstantial account of the prompt steps taken to fill up the vacancy in the Twelve left by Judas. But when James the son of Zebedee was put to death by Herod Agrippa I, no attempt was made to fill his place. The implication is that the death of one of the Twelve did not create a vacancy. Only apostasy such as that of Judas could create a vacancy. Any member of the group who died before the return of Christ in glory would be raised from the dead at the great day to inherit his inalienable share in the promise.

The importance of this is that it indicates that in so far as the Twelve had a special status conferred upon them by Christ, it was a personal thing and inalienable. It would be forfeited by misconduct; but it could not be transmitted to another. It did not pass at death.

It remains to ask, in the light of the foregoing discussion, what meaning should be attached to the words " apostolic succession." To what do the successors of the apostles succeed? We have seen that it is not the special status involved in our Lord's promise to the Twelve. Equally it is not the quality of having been an eyewitness of the foundation facts of the faith from John's baptism to the Resurrection. That quality ceased with the first generation of Christians; it also was not transmissible. What is left? So far as I can see, three things: the need of the world, the call of Christ, and the tradition of his ministry in the flesh in Galilee and Judea and in the Church which is his Body throughout the world. And, so far as I can see, it is the Church that succeeds to these things. The Church is apostolic because it is called by Christ and empowered and instructed by Christ to go and make disciples of the nations.

THE SETTLED MINISTRY

It was argued in the last lecture that the apostolate is not essentially different from the other ministries. The study of the Jewish institution of the *shelichuth* shows plainly enough the limitations that attached to this office, whether exercised on behalf of an individual or of a group. The evidence of the New Testament fits, in essentials, with that from Jewish sources. The men whom Jesus sent out during the ministry were *sheluchim* in the Jewish sense of the word. Formally they had the same kind of commission as Jewish *sheluchim;* what was new was the content of their commission. In the Apostolic Age the situation is different; but the difference is made by the exaltation of Christ rather than by the creation of a new kind of office in the Christian community. The decisively new factor in the situation is that the ministry of Jesus has been set free from the limitations of time and space which were imposed upon it by his human body. The risen Lord possesses an all-embracing power and authority; and accordingly his commission to the Eleven, as the representative nucleus of the post-Resurrection Church, is world-wide in scope, and in duration limited only by the " end of the age." Our contention is that the Church as the Body of Christ is apostolic in the sense that the apostolic ministry inaugurated by the Lord in the days of his flesh is continued by him through it in the new period of world-history inaugurated by the Resurrection.[37] The apostolate, like any other ministry of the Church, is an organ developed in the Body of Christ for the performance of a specific function, the missionary work of the Church; what in the commission to the Eleven is called " making disciples "; what Paul calls " preaching the Gospel." [38]

The result of apostolic work is a local congregation; and the local congregation, as part of the Body of Christ, itself enters into the apostolic ministry. This ministry of the local community is twofold: to proclaim the Kingdom to those who are still outside and to manifest the Kingdom in its own community life; to declare Christ to the world and to show the

[37] If that is the right way of looking at the matter, it means that we ought seriously to consider whether it would not be a good thing to dispense with the misleading term " apostolic succession," which carries with it the idea that someone has died and left his rights and property to someone else. Ought we not to be laying the whole emphasis on the fact of continuous life, unflagging strength, and unceasing work? And if we do that, can we find, and need we seek, any other basis of continuity than the risen Christ himself?

[38] When Paul says (I Cor. 1:17), " Christ did not send me out (as an apostle — *apesteile me*) to baptize but to preach the Gospel," he does not mean that baptizing is no part of the work of an apostle, but that it is not " first priority." First priority is the kerygma.

Lord's life and death and risen life within its own borders; to convert the non-Christian and to " edify " [39] the Christian. To the task of the kerygma is added the responsibility of *didache*. " Making disciples " is followed by " teaching them " the ways of Christ. In these matters, as in all other concerns of a community life, there are some who are marked out for leadership. In the Christian community the qualities that distinguish the potential leader are plain enough, for they are defined in advance by Jesus himself. Capacity for leadership is indicated by readiness to serve, that is, the ability to see what really needs to be done and the readiness to take whatever trouble is necessary and make whatever sacrifices have to be made in the doing of it. That very able and experienced apostle, Saint Paul, had nothing to add to his Master's prescription (I Cor. 16:15–18). So we come to the settled ministry. It need not be a whole-time job. It need not be paid. It need not have been to a theological college. Its only fundamental requirement is fitness and willingness to give the kind of service that is needed in the common life of a colony of heaven. This means teaching and example over the whole field of conduct: such teaching as is to be found in the practical sections of the Pauline letters, in Church manuals like

[39] And " edifying " means more than gratifying his pious feelings with nice sermons or appealing ritual. It means building him into the structure of the Church; making him a better, healthier, more efficient member of the Body of Christ.

the *Didache,* in apologetic presentations of Christianity like the *ad Diognetum* (v., vi.); such example as is offered by the lives of great men like the apostles or humbler folk like the household of Stephanas.

But more particularly the concern of the local community is with the ministry of the Word and sacraments, to which at an early date we find added what is called " the serving of tables," or mutual assistance. The ministry of the Word in the early days covers rather more than reading and exposition of Scripture. In I Cor. 12:28–30 we find among the organs of the community prophets, teachers, persons who " speak with tongues," and other persons who interpret these utterances. In Eph. 4:11 f. we have prophets, evangelists, and teachers. A consideration of I Cor., chs. 12 to 14, suggests that a visit to a Christian meeting for worship in the first century would perhaps have been a somewhat disconcerting experience for us who are accustomed to a regular order of service. One member might begin to speak to God in an utterance unintelligible to anyone else. Another might " prophesy," that is, deliver a word of God to the congregation. This word of God might be the announcement of an impending famine (Acts 11:27 f.), or a command to send out foreign missionaries (ch. 13:1 f.), or a symbolic action signifying that Paul was going to be arrested in Jerusalem (ch. 21:10 f.), or again a sketch of the whole course of future history to the Parousia, of the kind offered in the Apocalypse (Rev. 10:11). Another member might teach, by which we should perhaps understand the statement and explanation of Old Testament Scripture and the " oracles of the Lord," i.e., the words of Jesus. Naturally some members would be more active than others in these various exercises; and, among these, particular individuals would be more given to one kind of activity than to the others. But there is nothing to indicate that in the earliest days of the Church any member or group of members had an exclusive monopoly of *glossolalia* or prophecy or *didache*. On the contrary, when the congregation assembles, each member is a potential contributor to the service. One may have a psalm, another a piece of teaching (*didache*), another a piece of prophesying (*apocalypsis*), another some speaking with tongues (*glossa*), and another the interpretation thereof. All that is required is that each contribution should help to build up the life of the community (I Cor. 14:26). The ministry of the Word is the business of the whole community; and any member can take part in it.

The ministry of kindness and mutual help was likewise the right and duty of every member of the community. But in so far as the needs of members were met out of the common fund of the community, it was natural that particular persons should be charged with the administration. From The Acts we learn that at first the common fund of the Jerusalem church was in the hands of the Twelve. But very soon they asked to be relieved of this responsibility, and others were appointed and set apart to the duty. Later, when Paul and Barnabas are sent from Antioch with a relief fund for the Jerusalem church, the persons to whom they hand over the money are called " the elders " (ch. 11:30), and the mission of Paul and Barnabas is called a *diakonia* (ch. 12:25). Later still, the messengers bringing aid to Paul and the Jerusalem community are called the *apostoloi* of their churches. It is clear that at this stage the needs are seen and appreciated; that prompt and effective measures are taken to provide help, often at the cost of real sacrifice; and that means are found to convey the help to its destination. It is also clear that there is no hard and fast system or rigid organization for doing this kind of work. Each new emergency is met by an *ad hoc* arrangement. At a later stage we find these matters increasingly entrusted to regular officers of the local community; but in the New Testament things are still fluid.

Finally there is the ministry of the sacraments, Baptism and the Eucharist. From the nature of the case it is to be expected that in missionary campaigns the first converts at least will be baptized by the missionary; and we read of such cases in The Acts. In fact, we have no record there of any others. It is from the Pauline letters that we obtain further information. We learn from I Cor. 1:14 ff. that Saint Paul had himself baptized very few of the members of the Corinthian church. Yet he was in the city for about a year and a half, and it seems unlikely that no converts came in that whole period except Crispus, Gaius, and the household of Stephanas. We can only guess that some person or persons in the Corinthian community officiated when Baptism was required. The same applies to the Eucharist. No doubt the first Eucharists in Corinth were ministered by the apostle himself. But when he left, they did not cease. They became disorderly, no doubt; but they were still held. We can only guess that there was some person or persons in the community to preside. At the end of the first century we learn from the *First Epistle of Clement* [40] that at Corinth the celebration of the Eucharist was the concern of officers of the community who are called sometimes bishops, sometimes presbyters. Their office is called an *episcope*.[41] The *Didache* gives instructions about how the sacraments are to be celebrated without saying who is to officiate, except to remark that, when prophets celebrate the Eucharist, they are to have freedom in the eucharistic prayer. This document speaks also of the community appointing for itself bishops and deacons.[42] In the Ignatian letters we get the insistence that the sacraments

[40] I *Clem.* xliv.

[41] I *Clem.* xlii.; xliv. On the equivalence of the terms "bishop" and "presbyter" in I *Clem.*, see Lightfoot, *Apostolic Fathers* I. i. 69.

[42] *Didache*, x. 7; xv. 1. It is to be noted that presbyters are not mentioned in ch. xv.; though, as Harnack pointed out (*ad loc.*), they should have been mentioned in xv. 3, if they existed in the district to which the *Didache* applies. The inference is that in the *Didache* the equivalence of the terms "bishop" and "presbyter" still holds.

are to be ministered by the bishop or his deputy,[43] together with the clear distinction of bishops, presbyters, and deacons. But it is obvious that Ignatius is pressing for a fuller recognition of this threefold ministry by the churches; and the other evidence from the sub-Apostolic Age does not show the same clear distinction of three orders of ministry. The *Shepherd of Hermas* speaks indifferently of " bishops " and " presbyters "; II *Clement* mentions presbyters only. The letter of Polycarp to the Philippians speaks of presbyters and deacons (v. 3; vi. 1; xi. 1).

It is evident that at this stage in the history of the Church there is still a good deal of fluidity. The things that are constant are the real presence of Christ in his Church and the allegiance of all members of the Church to him; the Church's apostolic and pastoral task and the world's need; and the means of grace at the Church's disposal to fulfill the task and meet the need. Regarding the distribution of functions within the local community and the titles and status (if any) of those who discharge them, there is considerable variety of practice. What we have to remember constantly is that this is not abnormal and irregular: it is the natural and inevitable state of affairs. The Mediterranean lands — Asia Minor, the Balkans, Italy, Africa, Egypt — were the foreign mission field of the Primitive Church as really as China or India or Polynesia is for the Church to-day. By the end of the first century there were local

[43] *Smyrn.* viii.

Christian communities at all stages of development. Some of long standing were well established and generally competent to manage their own affairs. Others more recently formed were in no position to do so, and needed the care and supervision of the " missionary." The " missionary " in question might be a younger colleague of one or other of the pioneer missionaries of the first generation (a Timothy or a Titus). He might equally be a leader in the Church life of a more mature community (e.g., the Clement, who is the traditional author of the letter from the Roman church to the Corinthian). Or he might be a leader in a particular church, whose personal sanctity and wisdom made him the obvious person to ask for help and advice in time of need (e.g., Polycarp, bishop of Smyrna, who is consulted by the church at Philippi and writes to it accordingly [44]).

It is, however, going beyond the evidence and beyond the inherent probabilities of the situation when the attempt is made to derive from these pieces of occasional Christian help and advice a " regional apostolate," held by " immediate ' successors ' of the apostles," to act, it would seem, as a bridge between the original apostolate and the monarchical diocesan episcopate.[45] Nor are the cases brought forward particularly convincing. It may be that the presbyter who wrote III John " expects to control the *episkopos* of

[44] Polycarp, *Phil.* iii.
[45] See, for example, Dom Gregory Dix, in *The Apostolic Ministry*, 263 ff.

a local church "; but it is not the only possible explanation of the data. *If* Diotrephes was a monarchical bishop, the presbyter *may* have been a kind of archbishop; but it is not certain that Diotrephes was a bishop; he may only have been a successful ecclesiastical demagogue.[46] The descendants of the family of our Lord may have exercised a special authority over every church as Hegesippus tells us they did [47]; but he also tells us that their special position was due to the fact that they were martyrs and of the Lord's family: and, in any case, this quasi caliphate did not endure. Ignatius is put forward on the strength of his Letter to the Romans (ch. ii.2) where he is said to " describe himself not only as bishop of Antioch but as ' the bishop of Syria ' though the neighboring Syrian churches had their own bishops." But this will hardly do. The Greek should surely be understood to mean, as Lightfoot takes it, " the bishop belonging to Syria . . . the genitive denoting, not the extent of his jurisdiction, but the place of his abode." [48] Nor is the case any better in regard to " Polycarp, who, as his disciple Irenaeus said, was ' appointed by apostles over Asia as bishop of the church of Smyrna.' " This also will hardly do. The reference is to a passage in Irenaeus, *adv. Haer.*, iii. 3. 3, of which we have the Greek in Eusebius, *H.E.*, iv. 14. 3,

[46] On the whole question, see the admirable discussion by C. H. Dodd, *The Johannine Epistles*, 155–168.

[47] *Ap.* Eus. *H.E.*, iii. 32. 6.

[48] *The Apostolic Fathers*,[2] II. ii. 201. Cf. W. Telfer, *J.T.S.*, xlviii (1947) 227, " the Syrian bishop."

where the rendering of Lawlor and Oulton — " received in Asia his appointment from apostles as bishop in the church at Smyrna " — is surely to be preferred.[49] The other passages cited regarding Polycarp go to prove the respect which he earned during his long service of the Church and the extent of his influence. They show that he was in truth a father in God: they do not make him a patriarch in the technical sense. Finally it seems to be a desperate expedient when Corinth is brought into the " regional apostolate " of Clement of Rome. So far as I can follow the argument, it appears to amount to this. Lightfoot gave reasons for thinking that the succession list of Roman bishops is authentic and reliable. But there is strong evidence that the Roman church was ruled, not by a bishop, but by a college of presbyters, until well into the second century. Also the church at Corinth was ruled by a college of presbyters. Therefore both churches were ruled, not by bishops and not by presbyters, but by an apostle; and the apostle was Clement. Further, we are told, the situation is that " the authority of Clement the ' successor ' of

[49] It has the support both of the Latin version of Irenaeus: *ab apostolis in Asia, in ea quae est Smyrnis Ecclesia constitutus episcopus,* and of the Syriac version of Eusebius, which says that by appointment of the apostles " he became bishop in Asia in the city of Smyrna." Hebrews 7:3, to which Dix appeals to justify his translation of *eis ten Asian,* does not help him; for there the construction *eis to* with the inf. has its normal force and indicates the purpose of the appointment. We need better evidence than this for the theory that Polycarp was set up by the apostles as metropolitan of Asia.

Peter and Paul has been set aside at Corinth by the deposition of presbyters appointed by him. This letter (i.e., I *Clement*) is, as it stands, not merely a remonstrance but a recall to *obedience,* though a wise and tactful one. But it is not Clement, a leading presbyter, who writes as the amanuensis of the Roman Church [50]; it is the Roman Church that speaks as the mouthpiece of Clement, the ' successor ' of Peter and Paul, who is still equally the ' apostle ' of Corinth and Rome." I will say little about this except that it seems to me to show what astonishing results can be achieved when bad logic is allied with unrestrained fantasy. For the statement that the deposed presbyters at Corinth had been appointed by Clement, there is not a shred of evidence anywhere. The notion that I *Clement* is a recall to obedience to Clement, though a wise and tactful one, is an excellent example of the kind of exegesis that may be called, " Heads I win; tails you lose." If the writer asserts apostolic status and insists on his rights, that shows his apostolic authority. If he does not, that shows his apostolic tact and restraint. In either case he is an apostle. The third statement concerning who is mouthpiece to whom, so far from being supported by any evidence, is inconsistent with such evidence as we have.

It comes to this that we have good reason to think

[50] Strangely enough, that is precisely what Dionysius of Corinth thought it was (Ap. Eus., *H.E.,* iv. 23. 11). Cf. Lightfoot, *The Apostolic Fathers,* I. i. 69. And see Hermas, *Vis.,* ii. 4. 3.

that when a new local church was founded by an apostle, its first office-bearers were set apart by him, its first Baptisms and Eucharists were conducted by him. But we have no reason to think that all subsequent ordinations were held by him, any more than all subsequent Baptisms and Eucharists. Moreover, we do not know that all local churches were founded by apostles. Who founded the church at Colossae, for example? Presumably not Saint Paul, who from his Letter to the Colossians appears to have been a stranger in those parts. It has to be admitted that in the case of some local communities we simply do not know how they came into being or who appointed their office-bearers in the first instance. Rome is a case in point; and so are Colossae, Laodicea, Philadelphia, Smyrna, Alexandria. We know what happened in the case of churches founded by Paul and Barnabas, because the author of The Acts was concerned to describe the activities of Paul. We do not know what happened in other cases; and we are not in a position to say that what happened under Paul in one place must have happened in every other place where a Christian Church was established. It is, for example, possible that the " other *ellogimoi andres* " of I *Clem.* xliv., who appointed presbyter-bishops in the local churches when apostles were no longer available, were men already approved and appointed as presbyter-bishops in other neighboring churches. This would at least make a transition to the situation which we find in the *Apostolic Tradition* of Hippolytus, where the ordination of the new bishop of a local church is carried out by the bishops who are present, presumably from neighboring churches. There is no sign of any patriarch; and the bishop, who says the ordination prayer, does so by the *ad hoc* appointment of his colleagues.

The total picture of congregational life in its worship and organization down to about the middle of the second century is inevitably fragmentary and incomplete. And when we arrange the fragments, joining up those that will join, and placing as best we may the many isolated bits, one thing that immediately emerges is that at this stage it is idle to look for any hard-and-fast system, for rigid uniformity of worship or organization. We find some fundamental certainties which are the basis of all future developments of doctrine; some central acts of worship out of which will come the immense treasury of the liturgies; some simple forms of achieving corporate action which are the roots of the elaborated and immensely varied Church organizations that exist to-day. But even in these simple fundamental matters there is variety of expression. We find also certain persons who are trusted, looked up to, and accepted as safe guides, wise counselors, fathers in God. They may be apostles, like Paul or Peter or Barnabas; bishops like Polycarp; presbyters like Clement of Rome. So when the Gospel takes root in a new place, the young church there can look for guidance, encouragement, and help, it may be, to an apostle or to a neighboring and more mature church or to one or more outstanding Christian men or women in one or more churches. The nearest parallel to the situation is the modern mission field; but even this is not a perfect analogy, because the Churches that carry on missions to-day are highly organized bodies with a long tradition behind them; and they tend to impose their systems on the new communities from the outset. In the first century and the early part of the second, things were much more fluid, and there was a good deal of experimenting before detailed standard patterns of worship and organization began to emerge.

Such a pattern can be seen in what is now recognized as the *Apostolic Tradition* of Hippolytus.[51] This work, which belongs to the first quarter of the third century, may safely be regarded as giving the practice of the Roman Church in the latter half of the second. It shows us a Church with bishop, presbyters, deacons, and certain subordinate orders or offices: confessors, widows, readers, virgins, subdeacons, persons with gifts of healing.[52] We are concerned mainly with bishops, presbyters, and deacons. It need hardly be said at this time of day that it is necessary, in looking

[51] Here we are specially indebted to the late Dom Connolly's *The So-called Egyptian Church Order and Derived Documents* (*Texts and Studies* VIII. 4.), 1916, and Dom Gregory Dix's *The Apostolic Tradition of St. Hippolytus*, I, 1937.

[52] I give them in the order in which they occur in *Ap. Trad.* (ed., Dix) 18–22.

at Hippolytus' picture, to forget a good deal of what
we now associate with the three orders. Bishop for
us suggests the diocesan, presbyter the parish priest,
and deacon the assistant curate. But in the *Apostolic
Tradition,* that is in the Roman Church of the second
half of the second century, the bishop is the minister of the Word and sacraments to the local congregation. He is ordained by similar bishops holding
similar positions in other local congregations, after
he has been elected by his own congregation.[53] The
ordination prayer makes explicit reference to his
duties as minister of the congregation to feed the
flock, to " offer the gifts," and to administer the
Church's discipline.[54] The newly ordained bishop pro-
ceeds at once to celebrate the Eucharist for his congregation. Elsewhere in the *Apostolic Tradition* we
read of his function of giving exhortations and an-
swering questions.[55] In a word, the normal daily
duties of the Hippolytean bishop are precisely those
that are nowadays performed by the parish priest

[53] *Episcopus ordinetur electus ab omni populo; quique
cum nominatus fuerit et placuerit omnibus.* Dix, 2 f.

[54] *Pascere gregem sanctam tuam . . . offerre dona sancta
ecclesiæ tuæ . . . habere potestatem dimittere peccata se-
cundum præceptum tuum.* With the second of these we may
compare I *Clem.* xliv., where the presbyters at Corinth are
described as having " offered the gifts of the bishop's office
blamelessly and holily."

[55] Or possibly asking them; the text is not easy to
establish with certainty at this point. See Dix's ed., 47. On
the right to preach in Church, see C. H. Turner in *Cambridge Medieval History,* i. 161 ff.

or the minister of a nonepiscopal church. The presbyter's functions can be inferred from the prayer used in his ordination. It asks that God will " impart to him the spirit of grace and counsel, ' that he may share ' in the presbyterate ' and govern ' thy people in a pure heart." [56] The prayer emphasizes the duties that the presbyter has in connection with the government of the congregation. In the liturgy, however, we find something more. The presbyters stand with the bishop and lay their hands on the oblation while the bishop says the eucharistic prayer. This concelebration is important.[57] For the question is whether it is the first stage in the delegation of sacramental functions peculiar to the bishop or a relic of an earlier time when these functions belonged to all the presbyters. Ignatius may be called to support the former view and Clement of Rome for the latter. But let it not be forgotten that Ignatius is championing a new idea; Clement is stating the existing practice.[58] I have little doubt that we should prefer Clement to Ignatius in this matter, and that we should see in

[56] Dix, 13. With the prayer we may compare the sketch of the presbyter's duties given by Polycarp, *Phil.* vi. 1.

[57] See J. H. Srawley, *The Early History of the Liturgy,*[2] 72; G. Dix, *The Shape of the Liturgy,* 34, 110, 126, 590; L. Duchesne, *Origines du Culte Chrétien,* 5, 178 n.2, 467; J. Wordsworth, *Bishop Sarapion's Prayer-Book,* 24, 86 n.2.

[58] Ignatius, *Smyrn.* viii. 1, " *Let that be considered* a valid Eucharist which is celebrated by the bishop, or by one whom he appoints." I *Clem.* xliv. 4, " Those [presbyters] *who have offered* the gifts of the bishop's office blamelessly and holily."

the Hippolytean bishop a specialized presbyter, that is, one who acts as the permanent spokesman of the presbyters and performs regularly on their behalf the sacramental functions which at an earlier time they exercised in some sort of rotation. When, at a later stage, the ministry of the Word and sacraments became the main concern of the presbyters, it was not the delegation to them by the bishop of functions that had hitherto pertained exclusively to him; it was the resumption by the presbyters of functions that had originally been theirs.

The deacon in the *Apostolic Tradition* is firmly put in his place. It is emphasized that he is no more than the bishop's adjutant. He has no place in the council made up by bishop and presbyters. He has a special responsibility in connection with the charitable ministrations of the Church, reporting cases of need and conveying the gifts to the recipients. At the Eucharist the deacons have their duties in connection with the bringing forward of the elements to the bishop and in the distribution when they have been consecrated.[59]

But if the picture given by Hippolytus represents the state of affairs in Rome in the second century, it is clear enough that by the middle of the third the

[59] For the difficulties that arose from the tendency of the deacons to magnify their office, probably as a result of their close personal association with the bishop, see W. H. Freestone, *The Sacrament Reserved*, 223; Bright, *Notes on the Canons of the First Four General Councils*, Nicaea xviii, 59–64.

growth of the church is proving too much for this congregational episcopacy. It might still work in small places where the congregation was of a manageable size. It could no longer work in the old way in the Roman church described by Cornelius (*c.* 251–253). His letter to Fabius of Antioch gives the following figures [60]: 1 bishop, 46 presbyters, 7 deacons, 7 sub-deacons, 42 acolytes, 52 exorcists, readers, and door-keepers, above 1,500 widows and persons in distress (i.e., pensioners of the church), and an immense and countless laity. The laity is variously estimated: the estimates range from 30,000 to 50,000. It is plain that no bishop could be the minister, in the sense implied in the *Apostolic Tradition,* to a congregation of this size. Indeed, the mere administration of its affairs had already, before the time of Cornelius, called for the division of the city into 7 districts, each in charge of a deacon.[61] The liturgical service must have been similarly divided, presumably among the presbyters. Yet the whole immense community was still felt to form *one* church and the scattered celebrations were felt to be *one* Eucharist. The fact that the center of this one Eucharist was the bishop's celebration no doubt helped to foster the idea that the presbyters in the several city churches were only the delegates of the bishop. A similar result would naturally follow from

---

[60] *Ap.* Eus., *H.E.,* vi. 43. 11 f.
[61] According to the *Liberian Kalendar,* this reorganization was the work of Fabian (236–250), the predecessor of Cornelius.

the practice of sending the *fermentum* [62] to the city churches (*tituli*). The practical problem might have been solved by dividing the Roman community into a number of congregations of the Hippolytean pattern, each presided over by its own bishop. The Jewish community in Rome had done something similar, and we know from inscriptions alone of thirteen synagogues, each with its own organization.[63] But this did not commend itself to the Church.

The result was that the churches of the great cities came to acquire a prestige and power all their own. This same Cornelius tells us in the same letter in which he gives the statistics of his church, that he has just dealt with three Italian bishops who had been concerned in the consecration of his rival Novatian. One has been allowed to communicate as a layman on the intercession of the Roman Christians: regarding the other two Cornelius announces that their successors have been ordained and despatched to their places. No doubt it was easy on the morrow of the Decian persecution, when churches were depleted and shaken, for a bishop with the energy and determination of Cornelius to impose his will upon other churches in this way. But there is more in it than that. It marks a stage in the assertion of metropolitan rights which was going on all the time in the churches of the

[62] Srawley, *op. cit.*, 174, 233; Dix, *The Shape of the Liturgy*, 21, 134, 285; Duchesne, *Origines*, 166, 188 f.

[63] See J. B. Frey, *Corpus Inscriptionum Iudaicarum*, I, Introd., lxviii–lxxxi.

great cities, and nowhere more strongly and pertinaciously than in Rome.

Another development that seems to belong to this period is that of the *chorepiscopi*, first mentioned in the thirteenth canon of Ancyra (A.D. 314), but obviously in existence before that date. They have the supervision of the scattered Christians in rural districts. Lightfoot thought of them as a survival of the original presbyter-bishops. The more commonly accepted view is that they were more like modern suffragan bishops with strictly limited powers. Whatever their origin, they are a sign of the times; they mark the steady expansion of the authority of the city bishops, in this case over the rural domains of the city.[64]

When the process is completed, the bishop's parish has grown into a diocese, the bishop himself has become a great administrator, and the pastoral functions which were the special responsibility of the Hippolytean bishop are now largely in the hands of the presbyters. The presbyters discharge as delegates of the bishop functions that in the first century they discharged in their own right. One thing the bishop does not allow out of his own hands — the right to ordain and, in the West at least, to confirm. Thereafter it

[64] On the *chorepiscopi*, see C. H. Turner in Gore, *The Church and the Ministry*, new edition, 1936, Note D, 327–332; and on the whole development, Turner's Chapter VI in *Cambridge Medieval History*, I. I cannot help thinking that the letter of Cornelius referred to above has a bearing on the problem of the *chorepiscopi*.

becomes a matter of the great sees' claiming and securing patriarchal standing and metropolitan rights. The logical issue would be the acquisition of supreme power by one of the patriarchal sees; and indeed the claim was made, and is still strongly maintained, by the see of Rome. But its realization has been frustrated by two things, the unbending opposition of the Eastern Churches, and the great revolt in the West which we call the Reformation.

Episcopacy as it developed in the first three centuries was the only form of Church government until some of the Reformation Churches rejected it in favor of systems, presbyterian or congregational, that they judged to be nearer to the pattern laid down in the New Testament. But it has to be remembered that not all the Churches of the Reformation took this step. It was possible, and it still is, to be Protestant *and* Epicopal and apostolic. I should maintain that it is equally possible to be Protestant, non-Episcopal, *and* apostolic. For if the argument of the preceding lectures is sound, apostolicity is a quality that belongs to the Church, not to any particular form of ministry.

Churches are apostolic if and in so far as they have a call from the risen Christ to carry out the business of proclaiming the Kingdom and bringing men into it. If it be asked how we are to know that any particular Church is apostolic, the only answer is that where there is a genuine apostolic ministry, there you may expect to find the " signs of the apostle." If we can accustom ourselves to look for these, and, having seen them, to keep our attention fixed on them rather than on nice points of law about pedigrees and inheritances, we shall be well on the way toward that full and frank mutual recognition which is the precondition of mutual eligibility.

Nothing is gained by making for this or that system of Church government claims to which Church history is waiting to give the lie direct. Nothing is gained by trying to make debating points. When the Bishop of Oxford says, for example, that " whatever the schisms which have divided episcopal Christianity, they exhibit nothing remotely resembling the fissiparous fertility of nonepiscopal Christendom " [65] he lays himself open to the obvious retort that the major schisms in the Church, including the great schism of East and West and the Reformation itself, took place when the Church was under universal and long-established episcopal government; that some of the major divisions in England in the post-Reformation period have not been splits within the Free Churches but secessions or expulsions from the episcopal Church — the Presbyterians in 1662 and the Methodists at the close of the eighteenth century; that all the major heresies showed themselves when the Church was under episcopal control, and that many of them enjoyed episcopal patronage — the Arians were good episcopalians, and the Nestorians still are; finally that such effective attempts at overcoming division as have taken place in our day have mostly been carried through in non-

[65] *The Apostolic Ministry*, 13.

episcopal circles — Presbyterians in Scotland, Methodists in Great Britian, the United Church of Canada, the Church of Christ in China, the South India United Church.

But such points, even if they have to be made, are hardly worth making. They do nothing except prove, what we already know, that any form of Church government in this world has to be in the hands of human beings, and that consequently error and sin cannot be excluded by any eccesiastical constitution, not even by that *coup d'état*, the infallibility decree of the Vatican Council. What the Church possesses is not immunity from sin and error but the abiding presence of Him who is the way, the truth, and the life. It is promised, not safety, but victory. And, in any case, the positive achievements of the Church under episcopacy need no commendation from anyone. They are there for all to see, and they are, in the fullest and most convincing way, the " signs of the apostle." It is a long way from the superintendent-presbyters of the first century through the Hippolytean bishop of the second to the diocesan of the later centuries. But the living Christ has worked in and through that developing institution to no small purpose. Its justification is in its fruits in generation after generation of the Church's life. The same Lord has been pleased to work effectively through other institutions. Presbyterians, Independents, and Baptists, with some three centuries of experience of this, and Methodists with a century and a half, are not likely to accept anything less than the same full and frank recognition that they give — or ought to give — to the episcopal communions. The nonepiscopal Churches also can show the " signs of the apostle."

I venture to think that the real problem is that of finding a really adequate explanation of this immense and undeniable achievement of the divided communions. There is a tendency to-day to take refuge in the idea of universal defectiveness: " All are defective; but *we* are not so defective as some we could mention." There might be something in it if we could point to the notorious corruption and spiritual decadence that accompany Roman Catholicism or Anglicanism or Presbyterianism. But that is just what we cannot do. Our real problem is the success of the different Churches; and I believe that the way to the solution of it is to take the idea of the Church as the Body of Christ quite seriously. If we do that, we have to reckon with the corollary that there is one essential ministry, the perpetual ministry of the risen Lord, present, as he promised to be, where his people are gathered in his name, and renewing to each generation the gifts they need to continue *his* ministry. I close with a final observation. The prayer for the consecration of a bishop in the *Apostolic Tradition of Hippolytus* [66] is a prayer of invocation, and *epiklesis*. So is that in the ordination of a presbyter, and of a deacon; and that at the initiation of Church members. I should interpret this to mean that, while each of these has

[66] Ed., Dix, 4–38.

his own function in the common life of the Body of Christ, and while there are ordered relations among them of co-ordination or subordination, they are all alike in this, that all depend completely on the one essential ministry, that of Christ himself in his Church.

NONEPISCOPAL MINISTRIES

F OR those who think seriously about the Church and the ministry there are two main lines of approach to the subject. As an example of one, we may take the opening sentence of a book on the ministry by a distinguished French Roman Catholic scholar. He tells us that " the theologians distinguish, in the Church, a twofold hierarchy: one whose concern is the fulfillment of liturgical functions and the sanctification of Christ's people by the ministration of the sacraments — the ' hierarchy of orders '; the other which is concerned with the government and direction of the faithful, and is therefore called the ' hierarchy of jurisdiction.' " [67] This way of looking at the ministry is based on the conviction that Christ himself is the supreme Head of the ministry as a whole, " the sovereign priest of the New Law "; [68] and that all other

[67] J. Tixeront, *L'Ordre et les Ordinations*[2] (1925), 1. Cf. Loofs, *Symbolik,* i. 218 ff.

[68] Tixeront, *op. cit.,* 9: " *Le chef du nouveau sacerdoce est Jésus-Christ lui-même. Il est le premier et le grand prêtre de la Nouvelle Loi, au sacerdoce de qui tous les autres prêtres ne font que participer.*"

ministries are what they are by participation in his, while all other ministers hold office by delegation in orderly degrees from him. Broadly speaking, the power delegated to the Christian priesthood is that of offering the eucharistic sacrifice and of sanctifying the faithful by the ministration of the sacraments. In its fullness it has been granted by Christ to the Church, and it can be communicated more or less completely to individuals. The extent to which the power is communicated determines the grades of the ministry. The lowest grade has the least power; and each higher grade has the powers of the grades below plus its own special endowment. So it is possible by regular promotion to move from the lowest grade to the highest, adding new powers at each step without losing any that were previously held. It follows that the highest order will hold, along with its own special powers, all the powers of the lower orders.[69] That is one way of looking at the Church and the ministry. The ecclesiastical hierarchy is analogous to the military; and the Church is not unlike a well-disciplined army, in which the officers hold their commissions by delegation from above and not by election from below.

The other way of looking at the Church and the ministry is characteristic of the nonepiscopal communions. It has often been stated in words; and it has been worked out in practice in the Independent Churches, Congregational or Baptist. Its inherent logic

[69] See Tixeront, *op. cit.*, 53; *Conc. Trid., Sessio XXIII*, Denzinger-Bannwart,[15] §§ 957–968.

is pushed to the limit by the Society of Friends. Edwyn Bevan, in his brilliant sketch of Christianity, said that " perhaps the greatest contribution made by the Dissenters was the continuous testimony they bore, by their very existence, to the character of Christianity as a society to which men adhere by individual conversion and choice, not by birth." [70] That is the first mark of Nonconformity, according to Mr. Payne. " First, Nonconformists have insisted on the necessity of personal decision regarding God's offer of salvation." [71] The second point is " the belief in the Church as a company of believers, a regenerate ' gathered ' community, a fellowship of men and women who are consciously and deliberately endeavouring ' to learn all they can and practise all they know of the will of Jesus Christ,' a company of which Christ Himself is the head." [72]

The third point is the priesthood of all believers. " It has been generally agreed that certain individuals should be called out from the Church and set aside to be ministers of the Word and the sacraments, but they are not regarded as a priestly caste or order, able to transmit from one to another any special ' grace.' " [73] A similar conception of the ministry is stated in the Baptist reply to the Lambeth Appeal: " Our doctrine of the Church determines our concep-

[70] *Christianity*, 197.
[71] E. A. Payne, *The Free Church Tradition in the Life of England*, 144.
[72] *Ibid.*
[73] E. A. Payne, *op. cit.*, 145.

tion of the ministry. We hold firmly the priesthood of all believers, and therefore have no separated order of priests. The ministry is for us a gift of the Spirit to the Church, and is an office involving both the inward call of God and the commission of the Church. We can discover no ground for believing that such a commission can be given only through an episcopate, and we hold that the individual Church is competent to confer it. For us there is no more exalted office than a ministry charged with preaching the Word of God and with the care of souls. Yet any full description of the ministerial functions exercised among us must also take account of other believers who, at the call of the Church, may preside at the observance of the Lord's Supper or fulfill any other duties which the Church assigns to them." [74]

There are the two approaches: on the one side, the ministry conceived as a hierarchy organized from above, with strictly graded duties determined from above and carefully differentiated powers conferred from above; on the other side, the ministry conceived essentially in terms of specific tasks undertaken in obedience to a call of God and by the appointment of a particular congregation of believers. In the former case the emphasis tends to fall on orders and ordination; in the latter, on " calling." It might seem as if the two ways of looking at the matter were quite incompatible; that you have only to state the " Cath-

[74] Quoted in A. C. Underwood, *A History of the English Baptists*, 262.

olic " and the " Free Church " views fully and fairly
to see that they are irreconcilable. If that were so, I
confess that it would present as strong a challenge to
the Christian faith as I can well imagine. For consider
what it means. If the two views are utterly irreconcilable, it can only be because one, at least, of the two is
radically false. Let us suppose that it is the Catholic
hierarchical view. That system of ministry was the
only system of ministry in the whole Church for more
than a millennium. It is still the system of ministry
for the whole of the Roman Catholic, Orthodox, and
Anglican communions. Under it millions of Christian
lives have been lived and are still being lived; rich
treasures of prayer, of preaching, of hymnody, have
been given to the Church; immense tasks of Christian service have been undertaken and carried
through; men and women have lived saintly lives
and died martyrs' deaths. We believe that these things
happened because Christ was at work in his Church.
Are we to suppose that while he led his people in all
these other ways, he just left them to flounder in
error on this matter of the ministry? As the matter is
excellently put by Miss Carrick Smith in her admirable book *The Church and the Churches* [75]: If the hierarchical ministry " was a corruption, we must make the
vast and unwelcome admission that Jesus, who had
promised that the Holy Spirit should guide His followers into all truth, left Himself for a period of ten
centuries without witness as to His will for the order-

[75] 36.

ing of His Church." The case is no better if we suppose that the radical error lies in the other conception of the ministry. For we can point to achievements similar in quality, if less in total bulk, in the three centuries or so in which there have been nonepiscopal ministries in the Church.

There remain only two possibilities, so far as I can see: either the question of ministry is fundamentally irrelevant, and the Christian Society can exist and do its work with any ministry or no ministry at all; or both conceptions of the ministry embody some basic truth which can be found if we will look earnestly enough for it. I believe that this last is the only tolerable answer; and I believe that it is also the true answer.

In the three previous lectures we have been trying to approach the problem of the ministry by way of an adequate conception of the Church. I have been arguing that if we are to understand the Church we must survey the whole history of God's dealings with his called and chosen from Ur of the Chaldees to Calvary, from Calvary to the upper room, and from the upper room to the ends of the earth. What emerges from such a survey is a vision of the Kingdom of God — a Kingdom manifested in the mighty acts of saving power and gracious love performed by the King and in the loyalty, obedience, and sacrifice of those who accept the yoke of the Kingdom. This manifestation of the Kingdom in the lives of its subjects comes out most clearly in the Old Testament in the successive formulations, ideal or actual, of the idea of the Remnant, from the seven thousand who had not bowed the knee to Baal to the Servant of the Lord in Deutero-Isaiah and the Son of Man in Daniel. As that long historical development goes on, it becomes increasingly clear that the perfect embodiment of the Remnant idea must be, in the richest and deepest sense of the word, a ministry.

And so we come to the Messianic ministry, the public career of our Lord, a service so complete and unreserved, a sacrifice so perfect, that we can say of it, " This *is* the Kingdom of God." As it unfolds itself in the months that lie between the baptism and the Crucifixion we see it begin to draw other lives into itself. We see disciples apprenticed to the Kingdom of God by living with Jesus. We see the same disciples sent out as apostles by Jesus to spread his ministry abroad in Palestine.

Later in the upper room we see the beginning of the post-Resurrection ministry of the Lord Jesus. We see the birth of the new Body of Christ, a body which he can use to continue his ministry to the ends of the earth and to the end of the world. Of that body, the Church, he is head and life and soul. The purposes it fulfills are his purposes; the organs it develops and the powers with which it is endowed are his gift. Church history is the biography of Christ continued, the record of the life of the Body of Christ. There are failures and setbacks. There are some shocking and shameful episodes. They happen when members of the

Body rebel against the Head. But taken as a whole the story is a very wonderful one, and one that shows the Church as holy, catholic, and apostolic in a very real sense. There is more than a verbal connection between the " works of the Christ " (Matt. 11:2) in the Gospel story and " the work of the Lord " (I Cor. 15:58; 16:10) in the Apostolic Age. The truth is that the life of the Church is the continuation of the Messianic ministry. And we have to take that truth in deadly earnest.

But if we do that, if we deal seriously with the idea of the Body of Christ and the continuation of the Messianic ministry, we cannot just think of Church organization as if it were on a par with the political organization of a nation or the economic structure of a society: something that can be changed about at the whim of the electors. We misconceive the business in hand when we equate Romanism with absolute monarchy, Anglicanism with aristocracy, and the Free Church systems with democracy. These political categories have little or no relevance in this sphere; and what little they have can be expressed in the statement that in so far as Churches become political organizations they all tend in one direction — bureaucratic oligarchy. We are dealing with a living organism, which has grown and developed through the centuries in ways adapted to fulfill its function as the Body of Christ in the changing circumstances of its environment. The various organs that it has grown and the various functions that it has undertaken are to be valued in terms of their fitness for achieving the purpose for which the Church exists.

Again, because the Church is a living organism we cannot simply go back to New Testament times and say that whatever we find there must be binding forever; and that anything in the Church's life and organization that cannot be shown to have existed in the Apostolic Age has no right to exist at all. The episcopate, as it existed at Philippi and Corinth, and quite probably at Rome, in the first century, is indistinguishable from the presbyterate. A change takes place in the early second century with the insistence of Ignatius on the sole right of the bishop to be the minister of the sacraments. Later in the century the *Apostolic Tradition of Hippolytus* presents us with a bishop who is the minister of the Word and sacraments to a local congregation. Later still comes the development of the diocesan episcopate as we know it. Now it cannot be denied that human pride, human greed, and human love of power have had some share in shaping this development. (That is merely to say that Church people are human beings.) But we may be quite sure that if there had been nothing at work except these human weaknesses the Church would have died long ago. Even a modest knowledge of Church history will show the growth of the episcopate and other Church institutions as the response of the Church to what were felt to be the demands of its task in the world at any given moment. The final test in a living Church is not, " Did this or that exist in the age of the apostles? " but, " Is it here and now accompanied by the ' signs of the apostle '? " We may and must go back to the records of the ministry of our Lord in Galilee and Judea, for there the standard and pattern of the continuing ministry were laid down once and for all. We may go back to the achievements of the Church in the past for inspiration, guidance, and encouragement. But to set up the Church of the first or any other century as the final court of appeal, while professing faith in the continuing presence of Christ in his Church and the continuing guidance of his Spirit, seems to me to savor of inconsistency.

As another example, we may take the practice of administering the sacrament of Baptism to infants. We may look to the New Testament for a law commanding infant baptism; we may look to the Church of the Apostolic Age for precedents to justify the practice; and we shall look in vain. Infant baptism, if it is to be vindicated at all, must be vindicated on other grounds; and those grounds must be of two kinds, theological and pastoral. We must be satisfied that the practice really accords with our best understanding of the nature of the divine grace that is at work in the salvation of men; and we must be satisfied that the practice meets a real human need, which cannot be met adequately in other ways. I do not propose to discuss the problem further now. l bring it forward as a concrete example of the futility of thinking that every question in the Church can be answered by grubbing about in the New Testament and the apostolic fathers in a vain search for regulations and precedents, which either never existed, or, if they did, are now lost beyond recovery.

We have to take seriously the fact that the Church is the Body of Christ. That means that we are not entitled to ride away at need on the idea of an " invisible " Church. It will not do, when Catholics are confronted by the inescapable fact of the existence of genuine Christians not belonging to the Roman fold, to talk airily about the " soul of the Church." Nor will it do when Calvinists are in difficulties about the doctrines of predestination and election to distinguish between the invisible Church, consisting of " the whole number of the elect " and the visible Church, consisting of " all those . . . that profess the true religion, together with their children." [76] Nor will it do to distinguish between the local churches, which are the concrete manifestations of a sort of Platonic idea of the Church. The Church is the *Body* of Christ. That is, its place is here and now in the world of space and time. It is a thing, not an idea: a thing as real and concrete as the British Army or Imperial Chemical Industries, Ltd. It is *the* Body of Christ; not a particular body or a large number of bodies, but *the* Body. That is, there is one, and one only; and it somehow embraces in a single organic unity different parts — Roman, Orthodox, Anglican, Free — which are unconscious, partly conscious, or conscious of their

[76] Westminster Confession, XXV.

unity in the Body. It even embraces those who would indignantly repudiate the idea that they are united in the Body with certain others that they could name. The Church is the Body of *Christ*. That is, it is something that he has created and sustains and uses for his own purposes. He is not bound hand and foot by what *we* think he ought to do. He acts with sovereign freedom. He can use, and, so far as we can see, he does use his whole Body for the work of his ministry; and he does not seem to be nearly so particular as we are about whether his servants have been produced through any particular channel. The bread of life appears to be obtainable at Mass and at the Free Church Lord's Supper. Men and women are brought into the Kingdom by the preaching of Roman priests and Nonconformist ministers.

It is this fact — a fact which Professor Tixeront described in his way by saying that " Jesus Christ himself is the head of the new priesthood, the first and chief priest of the New Law," a fact which Free Churchmen express by insisting on " the crown rights of the Redeemer " — this fact of the supremacy of Christ, the only King and Head of the Church, that constitutes the essential basis of agreement for all the divided communions that belong to the Body. We talk glibly about " our unhappy divisions "; but, in truth, so long as we are under one supreme Head, our divisions must remain essentially unreal.

I cannot show this point more clearly than by quoting at length from " A Charge to the Church at

Its Minister's Ordination " [77] given by Bernard Manning:

" Let me then first remind you of what it is that you are doing to-day as you ordain your pastor to the sacred ministry of the Word and the Sacraments in Christ's Church. You are not to consider yourselves as having bestowed rather a pretty compliment on him in choosing him to be one of your ministers. You are not to consider yourselves as delegating to him, because you judge him likely to be reasonably competent, certain duties which (if you were not such busy and important people) you ought in truth to do for the Saviour yourselves. The sacred ministry in the Church of God is not a secretaryship, a sort of general manager's job, a device to save trouble for the majority of the Church members by concentrating nearly all their duties upon one or two. You cannot ordain a minister as you appoint a professional at a golf club or an errand boy in a shop. In one way it is true that our brother is to be your minister, but in a far deeper and more important way he is a minister of the Word and the Sacraments, a minister of the Gospel, a minister of Christ. From the Word that he preaches, from the Sacraments that he administers, from the Gospel that he sets forth, from Christ Whom he serves — from these first and most, from you in only a secondary way — he derives the power and the unction and the grace with which we pray to-day that his ministry is to be marked.

[77] B. L. Manning, *A Layman in the Ministry*, 152–160.

"Do not then flatter yourselves. Do not deceive yourselves. I know Congregational churches well enough to know how grossly they do sometimes flatter and deceive themselves in this matter. The things that make a man a good minister of Jesus Christ come from God most high: you can neither bestow them nor take them away. The weakness or the strength, the coldness or the devotion of the Church that ordains, as you ordain to-night, affect not in the least the validity or the fullness of the august commission that a minister receives. At your hands indeed he receives the commission; but it is Christ's commission, not yours; and it comes from Christ, not you. When your minister speaks, mark whose word it is that he speaks. You do not hear from him an echo of your own voice. It is the Word of God that he proclaims, no word that you have committed to him to-night. The minister is not the creation of the Church. The Church is sometimes his creation.

" So much it was proper to say to give adequate ground for your humility. But you are not to evade responsibility by pleading humility. Christ, the Head of the Church, it is who calls and commissions His ministers: but how does He do it? Through you. By you, the men and women here, Christ has chosen to make His call to the minister effectual and complete. Having said (I hope clearly) what you do not do, let me say as clearly what it is that you do. It is you who ordain. Other ministers present here merely represent you. You exercise to-night what is almost the solemnest of all the functions that the Church can exercise; and I remind you of it because at the present time it is challenged and denied. What is the heart of the difficulty in all these long-drawn negotiations about unity between our Churches and the Anglican body? It is precisely this: have you, or have you not, the power of ordaining to the Ministry? In standing out for the validity and regularity of their Orders — I use the language of the Anglican body — in declining to be reordained by bishops, who have precisely the same commission from Christ as themselves, our ministers are not fighting for their own dignity, they are defending your right, your right as Christ's Body militant here on earth, to ordain the men whom He calls. Make no mistake about it. No bishop, no archbishop, no pope can do more for your minister than you have done to-night. You have conferred on him all that the holy catholic Church can confer: Christ's own commission, ' Feed My lambs, Feed My sheep.' He is a minister not of this but of the universal Church. God forbid that any one of us, fathers and brethren, should ever deny that we have received and done what to-night we receive and do."

I hesitate to praise those words. I only hope that my quoting them may induce any here who are not familiar with the whole of that searching, cleansing utterance to read it for themselves, and not only it but also the other grand things that Bernard Manning gave to the whole Church before, all too soon, he was taken from us. Even more do I hesitate to criticize

or question. Yet there is one thing that disturbs me.
" You have conferred on him all that the holy catholic
Church can confer. . . . He is a minister not of this
but of the universal Church." And again: " It is you
who ordain. Other ministers present here merely represent you." I confess myself puzzled. For it seems
to me that to state the matter thus comes perilously
near to claiming for the local congregation rights that
we very properly deny when they are claimed for the
Papacy. In this account of the matter the universal
Church is an intellectual abstraction. It is not represented at the ordination. The other ministers present,
we are explicitly told, are the representatives of the
local church. I cannot but think that this is to push the
autonomy of the local church, and its autarchy too,
beyond anything that is warranted either by the Bible
or by the history of the Church. If the minister is
ordained to the ministry of the universal Church, it
follows inescapably that any ministers who take part
do so as ministers of the universal Church, which is
what they are by their own ordination. To call them
the representatives of the local church is merely to
camouflage the fact that they are spectators of a trans-
action which could be done just as effectively if they
were not there. I venture, with great humility, to
suggest that there is a serious problem here, which
Independents have to solve — the problem whether
congregational omnipotence and omnicompetence can
survive unmodified along with the real recognition of

the existence and effective functioning of *the* Body of Christ of which all congregations are part.

That there is an increasing awareness of this problem among Congregationalists is one of the encouraging features in the present situation. We can refer, for example, to the statement of the case made by Principal H. Cunliffe-Jones [78]:

" My concern for a new awareness of the meaning of a covenant is not limited to the local Church. I want to see a covenant for the County Union. It is precisely at this point that R. W. Dale's *Manual of Congregational Principles* is halting and unsatisfactory. I wonder if you remember the line of Dale's five principles:

" It is the will of Christ that all those who believe in Him should be organised into Churches.

" In every Christian Church the will of Christ is the Supreme Authority.

" It is the will of Christ that all the members of a Christian Church should be Christians.

" By the will of Christ all the members of a Christian Church are directly responsible to Him for maintaining His Authority in the Church.

" By the will of Christ every Society of Christians organised for Christian Worship, Instruction, and Fellowship is a Christian Church, and is independent of external control."

[78] *The Yorkshire Congregational Year Book*, 1947–1948, 15.

It is in his last point that Dale's argument breaks down. He has no theory of the relation of one Church to others, and he has not thought about the meaning of the word " external." Is one Church acknowledging the supreme authority of Christ wholly external to another Church which also acknowledges the supreme authority of Christ? Surely not. Anglicans use the term " Congregationalism " to indicate the living of a Church to itself without regard to the wider life of the Church. But this is a perversion, not a true Church order. In times of persecution a local church may have to live by its own resources. But in times of peace a local church has an obligation to care for the well-being of the whole Church throughout the world and especially for the churches of its own order. So I would add to Dale's *Congregational Principles* a sixth:

" By the will of Christ every Christian Church has an obligation to care for and be in fellowship with other Christian Churches."

In practice, of course, we have largely recognized this, but we have not brought it to explicit religious focus. That is why we should do well to recognize at the heart of our County Union a covenantal obligation of churches to care for one another. It is by the will of Christ that our churches are gathered into a County Union to fulfill their responsibility to one another in love and service.

On the other hand there is no call to sacrifice the

rights and privileges of the local congregation merely in order to enhance the power and prestige of some other bit of Christ's Body. It is not for the little finger to say of the big toe: " It must increase; I must decrease." There is no place in the Body of Christ for the domination of any single part: there is room only for the domination of Christ. There is one Lord and there is one essential ministry — his. All other ministries, apostles, prophets, teachers, evangelists, bishops, presbyters, deacons, are derivative, functional, and dependent on him.

What, then, happens in any ordination? Two factors are involved. First and vitally essential is the call and appointment of the minister by Christ. This is the one necessary and sufficient condition of ministry: necessary because every genuine ministry is Christ's gift to the Church; sufficient because Christ is the source of all authority and power. We have to acknowledge that it is quite possible that men and women may be given to the Church by Christ, whom the Church will refuse to accept on any terms. So long as it is in the world it cannot be entirely free from ignorance and sin; and it is still possible for the prophets to be stoned, and for Christ's messengers to be rejected and even killed by the Church. That is no abstract possibility: it has happened. The first and essential factor in ministry is the giving by Christ to the Church of the man whom he has called to the ministry. The second is the acceptance of Christ's gift by the Church and the formal recognition of the

man whom the Lord has called. In the Church this
recognition may be given by bishops, or a presbytery,
or the local congregation. We call it ordination. What
does the ordaining body do? It accepts the offered
gift, having first taken steps to assure itself that it
is a real gift from the Lord. It is possible for men
to be mistaken about their vocation as well as for
the Church to reject men truly sent by Christ. There
is no infallible touchstone under any system to decide
who are genuinely sent by Christ and who are not.
We can only do our best. By accepting him the ordaining body also recognizes him as belonging to the
order of ministers of the Word and sacraments, than
which there is no higher ministry. This recognition is
a formal and solemn act of the Church, in which the
will of the ordinand and the will of the Church are
united in an act of dedication to the service of God
and man, and the divine grace is sought in prayer.
The Lord who has called his servant is asked to equip
him for his task. It is the experience of the Church
that this prayer does not go unanswered, whether it
is made by a bishop, or the moderator of a presbytery,
or someone speaking for a congregation.

What difference, then, does it make whether a
minister is ordained by a bishop or a presbytery or
a congregation? So far as his qualification to minister is concerned, none whatever. If he has been called
and equipped by Christ, all the bishops, presbyteries,
and congregational meetings in the world cannot make

him any more a minister than he already is. The kind of ecclesiastical acceptance and recognition that a man receives may give him better or worse opportunities of exercising his ministry fully and effectively: it can make no difference at all to the reality of his call and equipment by Christ. That being so, the Free Churches cannot, without disloyalty so shameful as to be unthinkable, compromise on the question of their orders. We must go on insisting that nothing less than full and frank mutual recognition will meet the case. We should be prepared to accept any form of recognition and acceptance by another communion, so long as it does not purport to do what is already done or to make us what we already are, ministers of the Word and sacraments.

But let us not forget why we are able to take this stand. It is solely because we hold a high doctrine of the Church as the Body of Christ. It is because we believe in the real presence of Christ in his Church that we deny that any particular man or group of men is essential to an ordination. The Christ, who is for us the only and ever-present King and Head of the Church, is the Maker of ministers; and he needs no vicar to act for him.

It is at this point that I see the possibility of reconciling the two different views of the ministry. However much they diverge on everything else, they are at one on this point of the supremacy of Christ in his Church and his real presence in his Church. If all the implications of that central fact could be ruthlessly worked out and unflinchingly accepted, we should be well on the way to such unity of the spirit in the bond of peace as would take our breath away.

We should also be able to take a more unprejudiced view of ecclesiastical institutions other than our own, to see more clearly the full possibilities of a congregational meeting, the real value of presbytery or the episcopate. We should be in fact a good deal freer than we now are. Historically the word " Free " in Free Church has tended to be construed with the preposition " from." We were to be " free from " State control, episcopal control, presbyterial control. (If we carry the process far enough we cannot escape from the question: Why not also free from congregational control? Might not the logical issue be family worship?) It was probably inevitable that it should happen in this way; but it is not inevitable that it should always be thus. Freedom from alien control is still a good thing; and we must defend it at all costs. But it is not everything. We must increasingly insist on " freedom for." Freedom for what? Freedom to be the most efficient instrument possible for the fulfillment of the purposes of Christ. The Church needs to be free from other controls and ties in order that it may be totally obedient to Christ, fully responsive to the impulses of his Spirit. What form or forms of ecclesiastical organization will most perfectly achieve this aim is a question to be discussed solely on its merits — once we have come to recognize the proper place and value of ecclesiastical organization. We shall be able to ask what is right with other communions, not what is wrong. We shall look for things they have that we lack. Reunion will be a business not so much of sinking differences as of sharing our treasures.

EPILOGUE

IT is perhaps hardly necessary at this point to state once again the main contentions of these lectures. Yet I should not like to leave the subject without stating once more as plainly and bluntly as possible the main theses which I have been trying to defend. They are:

1. That the Church is the Body of Christ and the continuation of the Incarnation or, as I should prefer to express it, the Church's ministry is a continuation of the Messianic ministry of Jesus.
2. There is only one " essential ministry " in the Church, the perpetual ministry of the risen and ever-present Lord himself.
3. All other ministries are derivative, dependent, and functional.
4. All ministries are functions exercised by the Body of Christ through organs which are organs of the Body. Consequently it is the Church that is apostolic, and the apostle is an organ of the Church.
5. The things that validate any ministry are:

    a. The call of Christ and the gift of his Spirit.

    b. Those things that may be grouped under the head " the signs of an apostle." The part of ecclesiastical authority in the ordering of the ministry is that of recognizing and accepting the gift of Christ to his Church.

6. As the Church is the Body of Christ, it is one in virtue of his ownership of all its parts. There is a deep sense in which what we call " our unhappy divisions " are not really divisions. It is legitimate to distinguish between the Church Militant and the Church Triumphant, but it is not legitimate to distinguish between the Church Visible and the Church Invisible, or between the Church and the " soul of the Church." There is only one Body of Christ.

7. Therefore the true task of those who care about " reunion " is that of realizing more deeply and expressing more perfectly a unity that already exists by the will of Christ, a unity that exists in spite of divisions, anathemas, and mutual unchurchings, a unity that both transcends and defies these divisions.

The question that remains is the practical one: What is the next step? It seems to me that the thing that has to be aimed at is mutual eligibility of Church members and mutual recognition of ministries. Mutual eligibility of Church members means free access for the members of any Christian communion to the Lord's Table in any church of any Christian communion. This mutual eligibility is already in some measure realized. It is capable of further extension and it is of vital importance that the freedom to communicate should be freedom to communicate at the regular Communion service of a congregation, rather than freedom to join in a special celebration held for a more or less hand-picked group.

The problem of the mutual eligibility of ministers is perhaps more difficult. Here it seems to me that the starting point must be the measure of recognition that is already given by Churches to each other's ministries. In some cases the recognition is expressed in a positive statement, as in the case of the declaration of the Lambeth Conference of 1920 on the subject of the Free Church ministries. In other cases it is implied in the actual practice of the Churches concerned in accepting one another's ministers for occasional or permanent service under varying conditions. The most urgent need now is that these various recognitions should be made as wide and as full as it is possible to make them. As things are at present, the problem is how one can be a recognized minister of another Church without ceasing to be a recognized minister of one's own Church. I venture to suggest that the immediate practical task is for the Churches to devise some means whereby mutual recognition of ministries may be translated into mutual eligibility of ministers, so that, for example, say, a Methodist minister could officiate in an Anglican church, for a short or long period, without ceasing to be a Methodist minister. Such a form of recognition would inevitably have to be something less than " reordination "; but that is merely to say that it would have to be recognition of a ministry and not creation of one. It would be desirable that the form of recognition should be a single form produced by the Churches together and used by all in common.

Such a form of mutual recognition would serve as a transitional device until such time as the ordination of new ministers could be an act of a Church united for the purpose of maintaining one ministry to proclaim one Gospel.

INDEX